OLEG TCHERN

Alchemy of Pushing Hands

SINGING DRAGON
London and Philadelphia

First published in 2004
as Alchemy of Tuy Shou
by INBI World
Plochshad Borbi 13A/1
Moscow 127030
Russia

This edition published in 2009
by Singing Dragon
an imprint of Jessica Kingsley Publishers
116 Pentonville Road
London N1 9JB, UK
and
400 Market Street, Suite 400
Philadelphia, PA 19106, USA

www.singing-dragon.com

Library of Congress Cataloging in Publication Data
A CIP catalog record for this book is available from the Library of Congress

British Library Cataloguing in Publication Data
A CIP catalogue record for this book is available from the British Library

ISBN 978 1 84819 022 1

Printed and bound in the United States by
Thomson-Shore, 7300 Joy Road, Dexter, MI 48130

Table of contents

Editor's note

By Ambrosio Sambista

'Taiji is born of wuji (nothingness) and is the mother of yin and yang. In stillness, yin and yang unite; in action, they separate.'

Tui Shou (Pushing Hands) is generally thought of a means to enhance the practice of Taiji Quan. This comes about because it is a very effective practice for developing sensitivity to our internal state (listening) and for teaching us how to maintain postural integrity during movement. Thus, in Pushing Hands we learn how, in pressured situations, to keep control over the emotions, the circulation of energy, physical balance and structure. Of course, these skills translate very well to the practice of the Taiji forms.

We also think of Pushing Hands as an art involving partners or opponents, a fact that reinforces the notion of competition and its association with the 'external' martial arts. Pushing Hands often looks more like World Championship Wrestling than a deep 'internal' art, especially in competitions where the opponents are intent on defeating each other.

From another perspective, and one we will pursue throughout this book, Pushing Hands is a complete alchemical system for the comprehension, cultivation and application of energy. From this angle, it is a serious, utterly independent internal martial art with components of solo and dual practice, devoid of competition except in so much as we battle to achieve mastery of ourselves. (The partner is used to measure the truth of our own condition.)

With Pushing Hands it is possible to develop a fine sensitivity to our internal world so that what is outside merely becomes an extension of our internal reality, because we learn to act or re-act in harmony with any external situation, be it pleasant or otherwise, without losing our 'balance' or center. Balance, in this sense, is the ability to respond with confidence and flexibility to each unique situation and that is exactly the 'game' that is the play between partners in Pushing Hands. It is this point, the practice of learning how to control the internal forces in order to be respond appropriately to external forces, that makes Pushing Hands such a valuable tool in our development both as human beings and as martial artists.

How do we develop balance? Balance is an internal state directly related to the development of one's energy. Energy can be manufactured and stored in the body, principally in the three energy centers (dantian). If you are just beginning to practice the internal martial arts, the 'center' is your lower abdomen, more or less a physical location to which you should invariably bring your attention. To an advanced practitioner the 'center' is a kind of energetic structure (a 'knotted' form) which is actively engaged in controlling and issuing force. Both cases rely on the structure of the body and energy; in the first case the structure of the body is the precursor to structuring the energy, but the body cannot be structured until the energy has 'form'. To maintain our physical structure the body must be full of energy, because the 'root', or the body's structural integrity, is only created when the energetic 'vessels' of the body are irrigated with energy and interconnected, thus unifying the body both energetically and physically.

To fill the body with energy we need to know what is required. The entire process of learning this art integrates body, mind and energy, and because it is a complete system we are able to map the entire process and therefore approach our practice with a plan. With a plan we begin by knowing when to start.

When to start? This is an interesting question and no doubt opinions vary from teacher to teacher. But if you look at the entirety of Daoist alchemical techniques and Daoist philosophy, we can clearly see that there is a profound body of systematized knowledge and that the natural laws of Daoist philosophy indicate that there are fortuitous times for a thing's beginning. We tend not to sow seed at the start of winter but when the warmth of the sun promotes growth. In other words, there are times when our best efforts seem to yield no results and times when everything seems to fall into place. When things fall into place we sense that there is a harmony and order of which we are a part. We might allude to the necessity of preparing the soil before planting the seed in order to obtain the heaviest yield. So prepare the things that will promote the healthiest growth. This can be the environment of practice; free of distraction, full of nature energy, comfortable clothing (made of natural fibers such as hemp), flat soled, light shoes, an empty stomach, an inner smile and deep concentration, but most importantly regular practice.

It is our hope that your experience with Pushing Hands can be made more fruitful by helping you to read the map of the way and find a rhythm that matches your potential. We suggest you examine each of your practices in relation to the whole of the practices you intend to work with. Each of the Daoist internal martial arts such as Taiji Quan or Bagua Zhang is a complete system within itself. For some, one of these systems will consume all their interest. But we must ask ourselves why, if any one of these systems is a complete path of personal development, there are different practices within the same genus of internal arts. The reason is that each practice has a function to fulfill within the overall alchemical process or work with one's energy. Although all these arts are complete systems within themselves, there are significant elements which differentiate them. Knowing the purpose for these differences allows us to understand energetic work more deeply, and hence define and refine our practice routine to ensure our continued enjoyment of this path over the long term.

What are these differences? Taiji Quan is a practice which fills the body with energy, Bagua Zhang is a practice which constructs the body, Xing Yi Quan is a practice which develops the control of energy, and Daoist meditation is a practice to open and connect the energy centers of the body. Yes, it is possible to accomplish this in a single practice, but by combining these practices at various stages of our development, it is our opinion that a more stable foundation can be created by combining these arts, an approach which, at the end of the day, may allow for some irregularities in some of these practices that might otherwise impair our development, should one practice be our only route. The choice is yours.

So to return to our question, when is the most fortuitous time to commence the practice? It's simple really, you have already started; take your time.

If you are new to Pushing Hands, the starting point we advise is at first to practice without a partner. By practicing solo for a while you develop the ability to listen to your body without the distraction of another person. In time, you will begin with the partner and as you progress your listening deepens and you begin to experience and feel not only what is near, but what is at a distance. Ultimately, the whole body is able to 'listen'. Listening really is the essence of Pushing Hands, both as a fighting method and as an alchemical practice.

To 'listen inside' is a skill you can practice in any moment; make it a habit to become conscious of all your actions. Pushing Hands is always an engagement with ourselves, our own energy and condition. It is not the opponent who defeats us, but we ourselves.

In this first book of our series on Pushing Hands, we attempt to illuminate the principles of body construction and introduce you to four of the eight main forces used in the practice. Exercises for developing concentration and the initial solo Pushing Hands techniques are explained in words and images.

No book can be adequate for this endeavor. The tradition will at some stage require a teacher. You will find your teacher when your energy reaches a sufficient level. The key is consistent, intelligent and heart-felt practice. The concepts within these chapters are complex. Do not be concerned to comprehend all at once. Work methodically, one principle at a time. Keep the faith.

Introduction

The Relationship Between Pushing Hands, Taiji And Daoist Alchemy

Despite the proliferation of Taiji Quan worldwide as both martial art and healthy exercise, little attention has been paid in the West to techniques and practices seen as being adjacent to Taiji. 'Reeling Silk' and Pushing Hands are examples of such techniques. And while Reeling Silk gradually gained recognition as a more or less independent discipline with its own distinct principles and sequences, Pushing Hands largely retained its association as a strictly integral part of the training for Taiji Quan routines.

Historical reasons behind this phenomenon are obvious enough. Pushing Hands has been integrated into a compulsory routine by most Taiji Quan families for many generations. While the importance of this technique, known in Chinese as 'Tui Shou', has not necessarily been undermined by this, it has nonetheless diverted practitioners' focus away from its overall significance. Currently, it is hardly possible to find any references to Pushing Hands as an independent practice in its own right and most literature published on the subject traditionally draws direct parallels between the practice of Taiji Quan forms and Pushing Hands.

But is it correct to merge the two great disciplines under a single heading? Taiji is philosophy as much as it is a framework around which practice and forms can be constructed. Taiji is a spiral which through multiple twists connects the Heavenly realm with the Earthly mundane existence. Many more definitions of what Taiji really is can be offered, and to a certain extent they will all be correct, as the 'Great Ultimate' (lit. Taiji) lends itself to a number of interpretations without distorting its nature. Similarly, attempts to reconstruct this Heavenly order by Taiji Quan families in the shape of Taiji forms are all legitimate approaches to studying and mastering it. On a broader philosophical scale, all Taiji Quan forms (routines) can therefore be seen as a systematic attempt to decipher or decode the mystery of Taiji and gain that intimate realization of perfection that is carried within it. The laws of Taiji describe a uniform macrocosmic construction of the universe, which in a way makes it difficult to deny the linkage between Pushing Hands and Taiji Quan altogether.

At this point, we would like to draw your attention to the fact that the concept of Taiji is derived from the teachings of Daoism, which predates Christianity by a few thousand years. If we wanted to submerge ourselves deeper into the origins and significance of the art of Pushing Hands we would need to view both Taiji and Pushing Hands through the perspective of Daoist Alchemy. Seen from the purely alchemical point of view Pushing Hands and Taiji represent different aspects of a single structure. If we view Taiji as a spiral linking the two realms of Heaven and Earth, then Pushing Hands describes the force which reinforces the flow along that spiral. When we shift ourselves away from purely philosophical notions into a more practical context of internal martial arts, we discover that, similarly to Taiji, it can become a framework with set principles, rules and steps towards advancement. It can indeed become a completely independent system that does not depend on the practitioner's ability or willingness to practice Taiji Quan forms.

The reasons behind this are relatively straightforward, Daoist Alchemy does not contain a single prescription or recommendation on what technique or combination of techniques must be practiced in order to reach the ultimate goal. There is a multitude of Daoist practices from different schools ranging from magical to medicinal, each suggesting its own path. Regardless of what the goals of every individual practitioner are, a set of tools is available to reach that goal, however complex or straightforward. When we realize what tools are at our disposal it is a matter of personal choice to decide which can be best applied to fit our purposes. What we do not realize is that while these alchemical tools have largely been in existence for centuries and still rely upon the same principles and laws as they did at the time of their creation, it is we who have changed.

One sad (from the Daoist point of view anyhow) fact of life that we cannot afford to ignore is that through centuries of industrial development the human race has lost many of its innate abilities and skills. This is especially so in respect of the human body and energy, which from the moment of birth is subjected to influences and pressure from the environment which may not always be well balanced and which do not always yield a positive benefit to our development. At some point in our lives when we realize the need to act and improve and develop ourselves we no longer possess the perfect internal conditions to take this action.

This is the point where Pushing Hands can be introduced as a system that can coexist naturally with our daily routine and fit harmoniously in the context of contemporary society. The current fabric of social interaction is based on contact with the surrounding environment — a complex composite of all events, objects, customs and people that we communicate with. Ancestors and legendary alchemists who resided high up in the mountains and followed a reclusive path toward perfection were much less subjected to external factors and daily annoyances than we are today. This did not necessarily mean less interaction with the environment; on the contrary, magical Daoism for example, was based completely on the interaction with spirits, objects and energy.

The main tenet of Pushing Hands is exactly that — interaction with the environment. However, in order to interact with some internal benefit, one must create the conditions for such an interaction. Primarily, this begins by preparing oneself for this opportunity (as we are generally unable to alter anything but ourselves). It is true that there are many paths for self-development and ways of finding harmony with what surrounds us; the main distinction lies in the practicality of the means to achieve that and it's natural integration into our daily lives.

The practice of Pushing Hands begins by preparing the two primary determinants of our internal nature: our body and our energy. So far we have revealed little difference between Pushing Hands and other Daoist practices — after all, they all involve work with energy and many include elaborate work with the body as well. Here is the key difference: in developing one's energy Pushing Hands teaches the practitioner to position one's practice against oneself, through the use of a partner. Most other techniques effectively deprive the practitioner of such a possibility by simply providing a set of principles and rules and leaving one to work with them freely, without any chance to check one's progress or the authenticity of one's achievements. Without proper supervision by a skillful and experienced master, any practitioner can fall into a trap of self-deception, misinterpreting sensations and feelings for changes and genuine achievements. In the worst case, one can lose a great share of the acquired energy, leaving one unable to assimilate it or see the mistakes in one's practice which lead to its loss.

By requiring the practitioner to work with a partner, Pushing Hands creates a mechanism whereby one can test whether what one has achieved is a genuine result or is a mere pretence. It can help reveal flaws in the body's construction and energy flow; test emotional response and the adequacy of a practitioner's state in paired work. The way the Pushing Hands system is constructed allows each stage to be reiterated and refined in concert with the preceding stages, rather than individually, thus rendering balanced and gradual improvement.

'Push Hand' or 'Pushing Hand' is a literal translation of Tui Shou, which is precisely what we observe during conventional practice. However, if we draw on the perception of 'pushing' and 'hand' in the teachings of Daoist Alchemy a somewhat different interpretation can be derived. 'Hand' is seen as a tool for the channeling and concurrent transformation of energy. For example, the art of Bagua Zhang, another famous internal martial art with roots in ancient Daoism, focuses on the importance of the palm, with the hand as a continuation of the palm. Since the hand is only a tool – that is, part of a larger mechanism – it only conveys the principle that energy must be transformed for a genuine yield to be gathered from practice. 'Pushing' can be interpreted as 'reaching out to the environment'. Hence, depending on what interpretation of the original Chinese characters is taken, the actual technique can be said to include a much greater range of actions than simple muscular effort supported by directed energy.

Coming back to our original idea of separating Taiji Quan and Pushing Hands we note that while Taiji can be seen as an art of realizing the environment, Pushing Hands is the art of self-control within that environment. This puts Pushing Hands before Taiji because prior to realizing anything, one must be ready for it.

It is beyond the scope of this book to delve deeply into Daoist alchemical teachings as they have been extensively covered by many respected authors in intricate detail. Instead, we will attempt to apply the basic foundations of Daoism (rather than referenced solely on Taiji Quan) to the practice of Pushing Hands. Unfortunately, it is both impractical and impossible to provide comprehensive coverage of Daoist Alchemy in this title. A few terms and notions may not be explained and we greatly encourage readers to draw on other works for clarification.

Steps And Stages In Pushing Hands

Although we have mentioned that the practice of Pushing Hands requires interaction with a partner, few would argue that effective partner work requires a great deal of self preparation.

Altogether, mastering Pushing Hands involves seven gradual steps:

1. Listening to oneself
2. Listening to the environment
3. Perceiving the energy from the environment
4. Interaction with external energy in a controlled environment
5. Interaction with external energy in an uncontrolled environment
6. Transforming the external energy from interaction
7. Controlling external energy from the environment

Work with a partner follows the Wu-ji principle: it starts from 'nothingness' – solo work – and ends in the same 'nothingness' – unique ability to interact with any external threat, motion or object without physical contact. First, the practitioner must increase their physical and energetic resources required for interaction, then they are ready to learns to construct themselves around interaction with a partner. This interaction reinforces one's energy and body and ultimately relieves oneself from the need of a partner altogether by being able to interact independently with the environment as a whole, and direct or control one's efforts beyond any limitations of the physical application.

Conventionally, when presenting Daoist knowledge, the overall process in the whole of the Pushing Hands system can be subdivided into three dimensions corresponding to Qi, Jing and Shen (qualities of energy). Altogether, this forms nine stages of energy refinement and formation. They are not directly linked to particular Pushing Hands steps, though roughly we could say that the first three stages take place for the duration of the time we need to work with the first three steps. Stages four through six correspond to steps four and five, and, the last three to the sixth and seventh steps. The first two stages (relating to Qi and Jing respectively) include various kinds of work with energy, while the latter three (relating to Shen) we describe in terms of our interaction with the external environment.

The notion of coupling two energy types (eg. Jing-Shen), can roughly be described as 'work with one type of energy through the characteristics of another' (for example, Jing-Shen equates to 'working with Jing quality though the characteristic of Shen')

Dimensions Of Three Energy Types

DIMENSION OF QI 气

Qi-Qi	developing Qi
Qi-Jing	capturing Qi
Qi-Shen	dissecting Qi

DIMENSION OF JING 精

Jing-Qi	reinforcing Jing, readying it for interaction
Jing-Jing	assimilating changes from within
Jing-Shen	refining changes

DIMENSION OF SHEN 神

Shen-Qi	slight touch generates strong reverse repulsion
Shen-Jing	ability to avoid physical contact, contact through energy
Shen-Shen	both physical and energetic contact are averted

The Book

This book is the first in a series of five books which will cover all seven steps of Pushing Hands.

The practice of Pushing Hands is a continuous and gradual process and strictly speaking there is no precise sequence in which exercises must be structured. Because in alchemy many internal processes take place at the same time or iterate with different qualities under different conditions, the content of this book attempts to outline the overall sequence of developmental process, rather than specify a step-by-step order which must be followed.

A number of conditions exist which must be created for the practice to get a tangible foundation and for the practitioner to build the practice upon. The first condition is 'Concentration' (Chapter 1). We are all familiar with the idea of concentrating and it is neither exclusive to martial arts, nor a skill that can be developed in a single step. In this chapter we discuss the eight types of concentration which must be created during practice. Understanding the nature of these eight can be undertaken through six 'efforts', called this because of the tangible and conscious effort that must be exerted for mastering various types of concentration. The first means to test one's concentration in practice is by applying it to the construction of the body, or more accurately, by 'Constructing the sphere of the self' (Chapter 2).

Until the state of perfection is reached we will inevitably have to continue constructing and improving our body continuously. This can be done through the 'Thirteen Postures' by taking either a passive or active approach. Thirteen Postures rely on the nine principles of movement, which are keys to enabling the proper flow and assimilation of energy. Applying various types of concentration to postures and exercises reinforces the body, and conversely, as the body becomes better balanced and adheres to correct principles, concentration rises and diversifies into refined states. Constructing oneself is a long-term process and its ultimate success rests not only on the ability to concentrate well and use the right principles, but also on the 'Rhythm' of practice (Chapter 3).

This becomes especially important after some period of practice. We demonstrate a technique for developing the waist which allows a practitioner to integrate and reinforce the first two stages. Once the concept of rhythm is realized, through practice and physical construction in combination with concentration, the practitioner will begin to generate more and more energy. To prevent energy losses energy must circulate, filling up the body's energy channels and vessels. But before that can happen the body must grasp the concept of 'Yin-Yang' (Chapter 4).

This concepts involves being able to differentiate between the dual nature of many internal phenomena, between physical and energetic power, between left and right sides, above and below. Yin-yang is a very broad concept and has been popularized in literature to include many real life examples so one should not have trouble understanding it on a basic level. Gradually practice will deepen and understanding will emerge, which will unleash secrets and the hidden capacities of one's body. Having gone through the first three stages and a realization of yin-yang it is necessary to step aside and re-evaluate one's achievements. No skill is better fit for this than 'Listening' (Chapter 5).

In effect it is an intermediate stage which can take place between any other two stages as it is important to review one's level and test oneself regularly to avoid mistakes or excessive attention being paid to something. Listening in combination with the realization of the Yin-Yang principle will in time allow the practitioner to distinguish between 'long' and 'short' energies (Chapter 6), which relate to yin and yang energies respectively.

We offer the Taiji ball exercise as a means to work with 'short' energy and the Taiji spear exercise as a means of working with 'long' energy. Having felt the difference between yin and yang and long and short energies, we can take them even further by looking at 'Li and Ji' (Chapter 7), the two founding 'bodies' (forces) in Pushing Hands.

However, even the proper application of Li and Ji creates a risk of being overdeveloped and the next step – 'Gathering' (Chapter 8) aims to reconcile and balance them. The energy must be intertwined in the dantian. That is the primary objective of this step, which, like 'Listening', is an intermediate process. As we primarily view Pushing Hands as an alchemical practice rather than a martial art, it is imperative that the practitioner is aware of the concept of 'Eight Forces' (Chapter 9) that affect the environment and practitioner alike. Force Peng, however, is the defining force and that is why it's very thoroughly covered in this chapter. Having endured the effect on practice of various forces and after initial contacts with the external environment a practitioner can proceed to test his/her ability to maintain body and energy construction principles with 'Steps' (Chapter 10).

Movement takes the practice to a new level and although in this stage it is the movement of one person, it nonetheless assists the practitioner in forming the foundations for further action (such as working with a partner). Two foundations exist: internal, that centered around the dantian, and external, represented by the feet. Once the foundation exists, further construction can take place without the risk of overload. Having mastered principles in motion, a practitioner discovers the nature of explosive energy outbursts 'Fajing' (Chapter 10). Using Fajing demonstrates to a practitioner his/her ability to direct energy to any point or area within the body. Fajing is indeed one of the most misunderstood concepts because of its inherent depth and its alchemical complexity. The discussion of Fajing will conclude the theoretical part of this book.

CHAPTER ONE

Concentration

'Impeccability begins with a single act that has to be deliberate, precise and sustained. If that act is repeated long enough, one acquires a sense of unbending intent, which can be applied to anything else. If that is accomplished the road is clear. One thing will lead to another until the warrior realizes his full potential.'

In this chapter we will discuss eight types of concentration and their uses, and the six 'efforts' which are exercises used to develop each kind of concentration. You will find images and descriptions of the 'six efforts' exercises and we also discuss the significance, use and development of the waist, the critical juncture of the body.

Why are we talking about concentration? If we agree that we want to create and develop our energy, then without concentration the potential of each moment and each movement is largely wasted. To assist us to develop our concentration we explain the eight fold nature of concentration and offer you some techniques to develop it. Even if you practice a concentration technique incorrectly, it is a good start, because it is the act of remembering to concentrate that is the first step in developing it.

If we don't remember to concentrate we will only apply the principles our body already remembers, which may not be enough for energy to reach the 'roots' of the work. Without 'roots' the body's nine extraordinary vessels will not fill with energy and without energy there can be no circulation and without circulation energy cannot reach where it is needed.

In the Daoist system and therefore in Pushing Hands, the body is contained within a sphere whose center is inside the body. This center is the base. A sphere with one centre has 8 axes (the eight fold nature of concentration). This sphere represents the perfect body where 8 axis (i.e. 8 forces – 8 trigrams – 8 types of concentration – 8 densities of energy) are fully functional and allow the body to 'rotate' around them with a particular frequency and speed (depending on force).

If two centers (i.e. two points of concentration) are created, this obviously gives rise to a line (connection between two points or axis) and since this line acquires functionality, it becomes a dimension. That means the result of divided attention creates a dimension which precludes the use of other possible dimensions (and accordingly axes) thus limiting potential. Consequently the need to understand the nature of concentration is paramount.

Eight Types Of Concentration

☷ 1. Single Point

☰ 2. Volumetric

☳ 3. Gathered

☵ 4. Circulating

5. Flexible ☴

6. Knotted ☶

7. Maturing ☲

8. Fulfilled ☱

1. Single Point

Earth Kun

Single point concentration is created in the lower cinnabar field (the alchemical cauldron) and is the most difficult to master. Being able to do so is proof that a person can gather all their forces and control the body as they wish. When you can connect all six efforts, you will master single point concentration.

It is not possible to defeat an opponent who has this kind of concentration; they are really unassailable, so much so that to the ordinary person they may appear to have supernatural abilities.

So we can gather from that, that it will indeed take a profound effort to attain such a state. No rush.

2. Volumetric

Volumetric concentration is the exact opposite of single point concentration: it's one that keeps everything united by simultaneously controlling the five extremities of the body, i.e. head, hands and feet. It gives one the sensation of being able to see and feel all, and act all in one moment. Therefore it develops the value of the body.

To achieve it one needs to keep the brain under pressure (effort). You reach this state when your body is filled up with energy, so that it feels like a sphere; one which can rotate in any direction.

Sky Qian

3. Gathered ('Art Of Assimilation')

Once you have constructed the body and can feel and understand the circulation of energy you will able to feel the sensation of 'gathered' concentration. The effect your body experiences is similar to diving underwater; as you dive deeper the atmospheric pressure increases, compressing the air in your lungs. In this case, the 'compression' brought about by applying this type of concentration allows you to go deeper inside yourself. This kind of energy explains how it is possible to connect concentration and energy. So it can also be called the 'Art of Connecting Concentration and Energy'.

Just as water is calm, the sphere of ourselves is calm in static postures. We use 'gathered' concentration in static postures because they enable us to fill the body's nine energetic vessels, whereas when we move, energy must flow. It is also the concentration we use to connect the inside with the outside, the internal with the external.

Fire Li

4. Circulating

This is a spiraling form of concentration used in movement. It has the potential to make one's practice more profound because it develops the ability to 'listen' deeply to your body. It helps to gather the body with the result that you can improve the circulation of the body, energy and brain. By 'body circulation' we mean the ability to move in a totally coordinated way. This is conceptualized as the

Water Kan

body with 'five wheels', i.e. two legs, two arms and a torso which are connected to each other very naturally, allowing the body to act as a whole. 'Brain circulation' means that when the body is 'open' it starts to understand what it needs to do. It's as if the brain is everywhere throughout the body.

5. Adaptive

Wind Xun

We develop this kind of concentration to cope with the unexpected. In a lot of our practice, we are anticipating the next move of a known sequence, but in a Pushing Hands competition situation, we have to deal moment to moment without a predetermined strategy, so that we respond uniquely and effectively to each nuance of change. There is no set pattern to this kind of concentration, it moves from place to place. It improves our sensitivity to the body. It's like when you throw a ball against a wall; you never know exactly where the next bounce will take it, so you must be able to exert different efforts in order to catch each bounce. In this way we are training the body to find, in each moment, the best effort for the desired outcome. With it we can create different effects to various parts of the body. For example, it is possible to make one part of the body hard or closed while remaining soft and open overall. A good practitioner can use this to prevent the penetration of blows to the body.

6. Knotted

Thunder Zhen

This kind of concentration is used to create additional force, such as 'fajing'. The form of this force is in the shape of a knot. Knots of energy are formed by the movements one makes practicing forms. For example, each part of the form of Taiji is creating an energetic knot. The force, structural integrity or stability of the knot depends on your ability to control your body and energy.

7. Maturing

You use this to concentrate energy at a particular point and sustain it there for a certain duration, as in the process of assimilation. This is an interesting kind of concentration because it gives you the possibility to feel strong in your body. When most people practice Taiji Quan they feel soft and flexible, but they may not have created in themselves the essence to feel strong and powerful. This is because if you only practice according to the structural principles you can only fill yourself up. This is the power of Qi. If you use alchemical principles this filling up is only the first step. The second step is when you can knot this energy and use this Qi in movement. This marks the beginning of your use of Jing energy, a real power that can grow without limit. The power of Qi is easy to feel; it is enjoyable and healthy energy, but unlike Jing, it is unsustainable and hence alchemically of relatively little use. It is like a satisfying meal, after some time you will feel hungry again, and come to depend on the repeated satisfaction of the feeling. But if you develop Jing, you can really change your body, mind and energy, and that becomes a spiral of growth increasing with each turn, whereas Qi is like something which has just two states, on or off.

When you really transform your energy from Qi to Jing, and can gather the sphere of your body, you feel powerful, and this feeling contains the seeds of further growth. Yet, at the same time your body is more soft and flexible than ever. The body starts to be like a pump, which feels powerful, but from the outside people only see the softness, and tend to doubt the value of your practice, but you will have no doubt. In reality, you are like a small snake that in an instant can transform into a dragon.

So when we talk about the concentration of maturation it means we can use it to stay powerful during movement. Or, we can say that we keep our energetic vessels full. In this way, when our body moves, it is like a monolith because each point is like a head of the dragon, and the dragon has nine heads.

There are nine dragons involved in movement. 'Maturation' concentration is the art of keeping all the dragon's heads together.

Mountain Gen

8. Contented

We apply this in Pushing Hands to 'listen' to the situation. When concentration is total, the sphere is full. It's an enjoyable kind of concentration and the type most people are using because it doesn't require additional effort. You only need to use your feelings and your internal condition; it allows you to enjoy practice. When you concentrate using your existing understanding it can only sustain what is already known, but cannot not break free of that to realize something more. From another perspective we can say, it shows you your skill as it really is.

Lake Dui

Six 'Efforts' To Understand The Eight Types Of Concentration

We should now understand that concentration is important and that to keep the sphere of ourselves we need to use all eight kinds of concentration. In case you've forgotten here's our definition again. The 'sphere of our self' means the internal construction we create during our work. Imagine the body standing inside a sphere: this represents wholeness, completion and connection. When we construct and connect the body properly, energy circulates in a spiral, starting from the feet and going to the head and starting from the head and going to the feet. So we have two spirals working in opposite directions within the body, a yin and yang spiral. This whole construction we call the 'sphere of the self'.

Now we must find ways to increase our abilities to develop the eight kinds of concentration and for this we have six 'efforts'. (We can think of these six efforts in pairs: right/left, forward/back, up/down.) When we talk about concentration this is just information, and though we use one kind of concentration just to hear about this, we do not in reality understand what kind of concentration we are using. People lose time in their practice thinking they are using their concentration, but in general this is an illusion. We do not mean to discourage or disparage your efforts, simply to state that concentration has more facets than you may have imagined, so let's employ the effort to enjoy the discovery of these extra dimensions.

Most people who study the internal arts understand that all activities must be arranged around the dantian, but until the dantian is created how can we organize our efforts around something that doesn't yet exist? For this reason we must use special techniques which help us create the efforts. These will enable you to understand deeply and meaningfully what it is you are doing.

The technique we describe here helps to develop the energy for concentration by using a heavy Taiji ball. In order to create the six efforts we employ 'short' energy. This is energy gained from outside. The sequence with the ball will organize a 'short' effort for your body. The weight of the ball must suit the gender and build of the practitioner, somewhere between two to five kilos is fine. For a male the ball can be about the diameter of a soccer ball, women can use a slighter smaller one.

Techniques For Creating The Six 'Efforts' With A 'Taiji' Ball

Before starting this exercise please prepare your body, brain and energy. Use all the thirteen principles to 'construct your sphere'.

The 'three connections' refers to the three cinnabar fields, lower, middle and upper. When you establish the three connections you are organizing the effort to find your 'Supreme Center'. Looking for your center must be a real effort; it is not enough just to imagine that the lower cinnabar field (lower dantian) resides a certain distance below the belly-button. Until you create this center, you have none, so what is there to concentrate on? Nonetheless, it is important to reach some real results and to do so requires a certain type of effort. Here we explain how best to apply this effort, otherwise you may just be waiting, but you will wait in vain, because the center is not the train, it is the station. When we build the station we have a possibility for the train to reach us.

In the following series of images (Fig1.1-1.3) the effort is directed toward connecting the lower, middle and upper cinnabar fields. Like most alchemical exercises there is no need to rush. Prepare yourself and your environment, think kindly of your body and the effort you will now make. Enjoy the process without internal or external distraction.

EFFORT ONE

Effort of Gathering the Supreme Center or 'Art of Three Connections'

Fig 1.1   **Fig 1.2**   **Fig 1.3**

EFFORT ONE
POSITION ONE
Fig 1.1-1.3

Connect feet to the abdomen (lower cinnabar field).
Connect palms to the chest (middle cinnabar field).
Connect head with abdomen (upper cinnabar field).
Position 1 works with Yin energy.

EFFORT ONE
POSITION TWO
Fig 1.4-1.6

Raise arms in an arc from outside
to inside. Note how the palms
change direction. This second
position works with Yang energy.

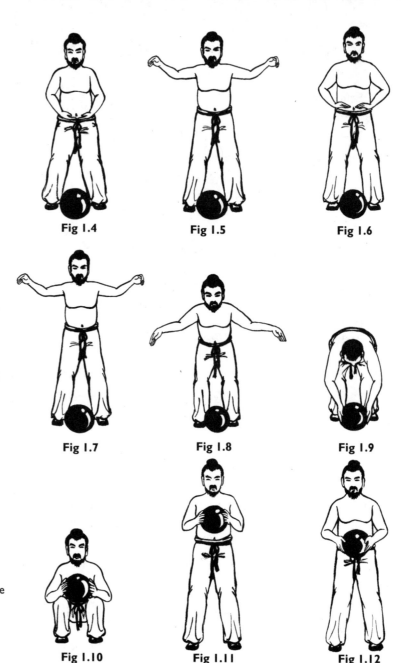

Fig 1.4   **Fig 1.5**   **Fig 1.6**

EFFORT ONE
POSITION THREE
Fig 1.6-1.11

Raise arms in an arc from inside to
outside. Bend from the waist.
Find the ball with the palms. Sit
back raising the ball as you do so.
Keeping the spine vertical, stand up.

To gather the three connections
we use the effort applied with the
ball.

Fig 1.7   **Fig 1.8**   **Fig 1.9**

EFFORT ONE
POSITION FOUR
Fig 1.12

Lower the ball from the chest to the
abdomen. Connect abdomen with
the ball.

Fig 1.10   **Fig 1.11**   **Fig 1.12**

Fig 1.13   Fig 1.14   Fig 1.15   Fig 1.16

EFFORT ONE
POSITION FIVE
Fig 1.13-1.14

'Creating Internal Breathing'.
Tilt forward about 10
degrees. Gather the abdomen.
Return to vertical position.
Open the abdomen.

Fig 1.17   Fig 1.18   Fig 1.19

EFFORT ONE
POSITION SIX
Fig 1.14-1.19

Support ball in the right palm.
Place left palm on the waist.
Using the waist, turn to the left
and right sides, while rotating
the ball around the abdomen.
Rotating the ball strengthens
the abdomen.
This completes the first effort.

The second kind of effort is defined by the two axes that help to organize the left and right sides of the body. The right axis is the connection between the right shoulder and right hip. For men, the effort applied in this position is working with 'small Yin' energy. It helps gather energy in their lower cinnabar field. For women, the right axis is working with 'small Yang' energy. It helps gather energy in their upper cinnabar field (head) and improve concentration in this center.

EFFORT TWO
Effort of Left and Right Side Axes

25

Fig 1.20

Fig 1.21

Fig 1.22

Fig 1.23

Fig 1.24

Fig 1.25

Fig 1.26

Fig 1.27

Fig 1.28

Fig 1.29

Fig 1.30

26

1. Roll ball to the right shoulder.
2. Turn waist right and lower ball.
3. Turn waist left and return ball to the starting position (center).
4. Change hands. Left palm takes the ball.
5. Roll and raise the ball to the left shoulder.
6. Turn waist left and lower ball.
7. Repeat this sequence three times on each side.
8. On the last repetition close the feet.
   Place the right palm on top of the ball.

For men, this position strengthens the 'small Yang' axis. Concentration is directed to and improved in the upper cinnabar filed. For women, the 'small Yin' axis is strengthened while concentration is directed to and improved in the lower cinnabar field.

Repeat this sequence three times on both sides, however on the second and third repetitions do not hold the ball on the shoulder, but allow the entire movement to flow from beginning to end. This completes the second effort.

EFFORT THREE
Effort of Rotation

Here, rotation refers to the ability to articulate and direct effort using the waist. The better your use of the waist, the more forces you can connect, hence more energy will reach the upper cinnabar field and thereby improve concentration.

1. Take one step back. Keep weight on the front leg.
2. Change weight and rotate ball so that the fingers are pointing down.
3. Turn waist left and rotate ball so that the left palm is on top of the ball.
4. Turn waist right so that the left palm is behind the ball.
   Prepare to push the ball forward.
5. Change weight and push the ball forward.
6. Turn the waist and return starting position.
7. Repeat sequence twice more.

After the third repetition close the feet and hold the ball opposite the chest. Concentrate on relaxing the waist. If your waist meridian is activated, you will feel the energy flowing, but don't worry if you can't, it's just important to maintain the relaxation.

...'the strength of the palm, wrist, elbow, shoulder, back, waist, hip, knee, foot, and upper and lower nine joints are issued from the waist. Without the use of the waist, high skill level will be difficult to achieve'.
Taiji Classics

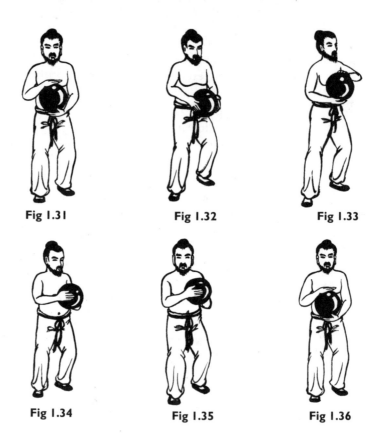

Fig 1.31   Fig 1.32   Fig 1.33

Fig 1.34   Fig 1.35   Fig 1.36

The Use Of The Waist

The whole sequence is repeated on the opposite side. This completes the third effort.

The waist is the juncture which connects upper and lower. Should this connection be weak, it means that the whole body will be uncoordinated and unable to manifest its power externally, meaning that your Pushing Hands will be relatively ineffectual. In preparing the body for Pushing Hands or any other Nei Gong art, the aim is to unify the body so that it becomes a 'single limb'. For this to happen we must fill and connect the nine energy centers of the body, or in mechanical terms, connect the nine joints. The waist is the major axis of this unification, which is why most students will begin by learning techniques to develop the waist's flexibility and articulation.

But what is the waist? Physiologically, movement is derived from the muscles, tendons and joints that connect the skeleton and the central nervous system that physically relays our intentions. There are 206 such connections between the bones. The bones which articulate to provide movement are the major joints (minor joints being fingers, toes, vertebrae etc), ankles, knees, hips, shoulders, elbows, wrists. These provide the major axis of movement. Therefore if we take the principle of 'the body becoming one limb' we can see the importance of the waist, as it is impossible to conceive of a totally connected body without the structure of the waist connecting upper and lower. It is the center of gravity of the body, like the hub of an axel, both physically and energetically. Is it any wonder that conception occurs and the foetus develops in this area? It is the point of origin of our very body and consequently of very great significance in alchemical or energetic terms. The waist encircles the abdomen which in alchemical terms is the cooking pot, the place where we gather and refine the ingredients of creation; therefore it is in constant touch with all movements, exchanges and transference of energy. In fact it is the mind of the body.

Unifying the body means that all extraordinary energetic vessels are full of energy and interconnected. If this is true then the left foot can connect to the right palm and stay connected as the body moves. The vessel which keeps the integrity of this connection during movement is the waist. If the hips turn, the entire spine, including the sacrum, turns and the rotation is in the ball-joint of the hip. When the waist turns, the sacrum remains still but the vertebrae above the sacrum rotate. The waist may turn by itself, but at no time should the hips turn without the waist.

Exercises which promote the development of the waist are many ('reeling silk' is popular), but even a standing posture offers so much scope to explore the web of connections centered there.

1. Open the feet. Try to feel the effort from the feet which gives rise to the force to lift the ball. It's important to understand that forces must go from below to above and that the effort to lift the ball is not a physical effort. To accomplish this you must create a spiral which connects the feet with the palms. The force must go through the three cinnabar fields. During the movement, the spine, chest and sides must control this spiral and prevent it from escaping.

EFFORT FOUR
**Effort of
Connecting the
Extremities**

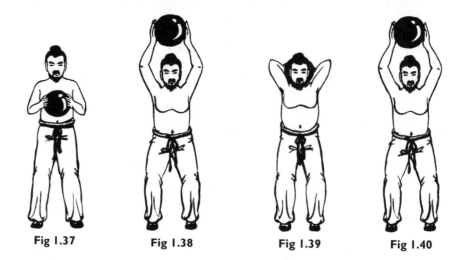

Fig 1.37   Fig 1.38   Fig 1.39   Fig 1.40

2. Lift the ball over the head.
3. When the ball is above the head lower it behind the head and put the energy of this effort into the lower cinnabar field and save the connection between the lower field and feet.
4. Raise the ball simply relying upon the force of the lower cinnabar field.

EFFORT FIVE
Effort of Forward and Backward

This kind of effort increases the force in the spine and the chest. When the ball is raised gather the chest, when it is lowered gather the spine.

Fig 1.41   Fig 1.42   Fig 1.43   Fig 1.44

Fig 1.45

Fig 1.46

Fig 1.47

Fig 1.48

Fig 1.49

1. Bend forward slightly. Concentrate on the connection between legs and the lower cinnabar field. Work with this effort without losing this connection.
2. Bend forward and lower the ball to the level of the diaphragm.
3. Gather the spine and push the ball up over the head.

This effort is exactly the same as Effort One.

After completing this, the complex is finished.

EFFORT SIX

Effort of Gathering the Supreme Centre

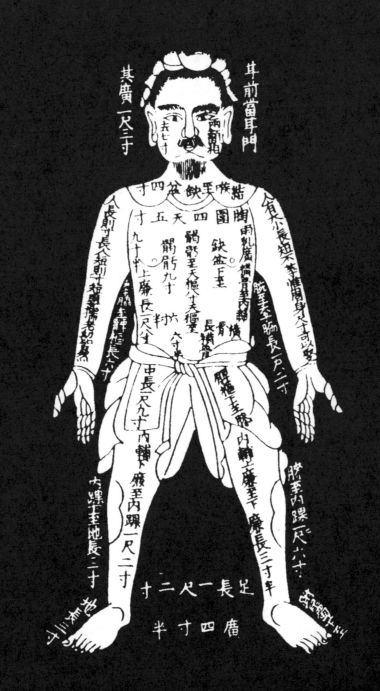

CHAPTER TWO
Constructing the 'Sphere' of the Self

The 'sphere of the self' means the construction we create during our work. Imagine the body standing inside a sphere; this represents wholeness, completion and connection. When we construct and connect the body properly, energy circulates in a spiral starting from the feet and going to the head and starting from the head and going to the feet. So we have two spirals working in opposite directions within the body, a Yin and Yang spiral. This whole construction we call the 'sphere'.

In this section we explore how to construct the body. We explain the relationship between each physical principle of posture and the energetic structure of the body, because the purpose of applying these physical principles is to ensure the integrity of the body's energetic connections. Therefore, each part of the body is described in relation to both posture and the circulation of energy. Various Pushing Hands sources describe a commonly available set of postural principles and this is a valid starting point, but the body is not just a mechanical device, it lives and breathes because of energy. A computer can visualize the body's skeletal and musculo-tendon system. We can apply all the correct principles and generate the perfect posture on the computer-generated image, but this 'virtual' body has no energy. Thus, it's perfect in theory but flawed in practice. This is analogous to describing posture without explaining energetic principles. The purpose of this chapter is to understand the connection between the mechanical principles and energy at a deeper level.

Also in this chapter we examine the ancient Daoist concept of 'Thirteen Postures'. These form the foundation of all Taiji Quan styles and forms, yet were discovered long before the invention of the Taiji form. They are the essential building blocks of all Chinese internal arts practices, being the essence and key to it is hidden power. By first understanding how to construct the body correctly, you will be able to extract maximum benefit from your work with these postures.

Following the 'Tirteen Postures' is a section where we describe the principles behind the 'Internal and External Harmonies' of the body. And finally, we look at the 'Nine Keys of Movement', a set of principles that will help you understand how to construct 'the sphere of the body' during movement.

Introduction

In this section on body construction we take each part individually, because in the early stages of our practice, we need to deconstruct the body into its component parts. By working with each part we can begin to awaken our sensations and once we can feel the individual parts, we can begin to connect them. Ultimately, each part will 'open' and your body will become united and coordinated. The 'sphere' will be formed.

From conception our body is formed in a spiral manner; bones, muscles, tendons and organs follow the current of spiraling energy until their final form is complete. This is also clearly demonstrated in the spiraling shape of the DNA helix. The explanation for this lies in the way physical matter is acted upon by the gravitational field. Rudolf Steiner postulated that liquid in zero gravity (deep space) holds a spherical shape but when gravity acts upon this sphere, it unravels as a spiral. Our bodies are composed mainly of water, and also grew under the influence of gravity, seen too in the growth of trees, which spiral out the ground as they grow, or water draining out of a bath. All physical actions, their force and flow, stem from this fundamental quantum reality, in the same way as do the formation of galaxies, rotation of planets and cycle of the seasons. We are not separate from this. This is a law of nature, and one embedded in the energetic concepts and every movement in the practice of Chinese internal martial arts.

In the beginning, it is easier to learn body-energy construction in static postures, such as qigong stances, but when the time is right, we need to work with techniques that will create the ability to maintain our physical structure while moving and changing direction. Obviously it is quite easy to lose the principles at first and even more so while practicing Pushing Hands with a partner, especially an aggressive one. To survive these situations we rely on our ability to keep balanced and centered and at the same time powerful and effective, and that is only possible when we have a real understanding of the mind-body-energy connection.

When the body is constructed it literally becomes like a single limb; torso, limbs and head are all co-coordinated; the centre controls the extremities, intention controls action. Movement, like good music, depends on the harmony of the musicians. The players, in this case, your body parts, follow the conductor. In the body, the conductor is the dantian. If musicians don't listen to each other, the music is discordant. If the body doesn't listen to the dantian the movement is discordant.

Let's give a brief overview of what we are trying to achieve in the first stage of our body-energy construction. The foundation of all movement is in the abdomen, the lower cinnabar field or the lower dantian, call it what you will. To construct the dantian takes some time, but until all movement originates from this energetic center, the three internal spheres or energy fields (abdomen, chest, head) will not be connected. If they are not connected the body and limbs are not working together.

It is especially important in the practice of Pushing Hands to apply this knowledge, the reason being that unlike Taiji where to practice without the foundation will only stagnate your progress, in Pushing Hands you can actually deplete your energy. In Pushing Hands energy must go inside our body and not escape outside. When we push, yang energy fills the body, and when we defend, yin energy fills the body, this is the alchemical 'secret' of this art or the reason why we say that it is way of self mastery rather than mastery over others.

If we apply both mechanical and energetic principles to 'constructing the sphere of the self' it becomes a method that creates 'Major Yang'. Major Yang is the energy of change. Changing our internal energy creates the possibility to improve or reconstruct the body. This approach energizes the mechanical principles with mind and energy. By bringing our understanding of energetic work and concentration into the postures we can realize the deeper significance of the postures and enliven the whole process. However, this 'active' approach is quite difficult to explain let alone be understood solely by intellectual analysis. Initially, one's body may better understand what the intellect can only dimly grasp; knowledge may be 'felt' rather than understood.

What we call the 'passive' method, i.e. one that uses only the physical or mechanical method views the process of body construction one-dimensionally. Suppose you look at a cube side-on, your perception is convinced that you see a square. Your perception is limited to one dimension, while the cube actually contains five planes or vertical axes. Likewise, a one dimensional perspective perceives only a circle when viewing a sphere, which in reality has eight planes or axes. The passive approach tends to reduce things to such a degree that the information is in fact counter productive. Thinking that you have all the information may satisfy the hunger for knowledge, but result in stagnation.

'Active' Structural Principles

Now, let's take those mechanical principles and fill them with energy!
Remember – all principles are keys to opening energy.

1. CONTROL THE VERTICAL AXIS

When we construct our vertical axis we can say it is a line in the spine, but this depends on what supports the spine. It can be supported by a single axis, just itself, or if we support the spine with the legs we can say it is supported by the cube and if we include our head (intention/knowledge/spirit) we can say it is supported by the sphere of eight forces.

We need to understand all these principles as volumes not as planes. But to understand volume we need to have created energy in our body. Without energy, any figure is one-dimensional.

In the passive/mechanistic approach to postural alignment we have only a physical notion of how to construct the body. In the second, or cubed, approach we have a notional construction using both energy and biomechanics. But in the third, or spherical, approach we have bio-mechanical, energetic and spiritual components forming a complete notion of what it means to 'keep the vertical axis'.

Unfortunately, the modern world has impacted our bodies from birth in such a way that we no longer have the naturalness we had at birth, so our bones, tendons and muscles must be 'opened up' again in order for the energy to flow and connect all nine energetic vessels. If the energy starts working it can fill our body, and, if it can fill our body we have the possibility to create our 'vertical axis'.

When this work is more than just a physical process, when energy begins to color the picture, then we have the possibility to create the 'vertical axis' in three dimensions / five directions / eight axes.

In Pushing Hands, the upper and lower parts of the body must be connected. This connection is formed by a spiral of energy which travels from the feet through the waist, via the torso to the fingers. By keeping the vertical axis we do not inhibit the flow of the spiraling energy. By keeping the vertical axis our body can support the spiral of energy.

We have tried to explain what can be inferred about the 'vertical axis' viewed from a spherical perspective. As you can appreciate, it is not as simple as just holding the body in a rigidly physical way. So we need to be careful when we think about constructing our body mechanically because it is a very rough interpretation to say we can construct the body on physical principles alone. As we said at the start, to realize the truth of this requires you to work consciously toward it; the reading of this passage is a long way from the reality, so take time to train and the result will surely appear. Once more, remember all principles are keys to opening energy.

2. TUCK THE COCCYX

Why do we tuck the coccyx under – to keep the back straight? No. We tuck the coccyx to turn energy back to the center, to the lower dantian. But, until you have energy to turn back, a tucked coccyx will not help. To change the body you need to create energy. When energy irrigates the muscles, bones and tendons, then you can change the body. If you have no energy then you are creating one destroyed body from another.

3. KEEP THE CHEST 'EMPTY'

This postural principle means little until one can experience the circulation of energy through the microcosmic orbit. So, rather than concentrating on forcing an exaggerated curve in the spine in the belief it will assist the passage of energy, it will be more constructive to practice the microcosmic orbit meditation. So bear in mind while you do relax the shoulders and keep the chest a little inside, the real art will be discovered in meditation.

The microcosmic orbit meditation works with the main front and back meridians, the 'governor' and 'conception' vessels. The meridian which runs down the back is the 'Sea of Yang', the front meridian is the 'Sea of Yin'. Doing this meditation regulates the circulation of energy around these meridians. If our microcosmic orbit is functioning normally so do the yin/yang meridians and organs, meaning that energy will be distributed to all parts and all nine vessels will be filled with energy, the most important vessel being the 'Golden Flower'. In this case we have the possibility to transform our energy.

4. CONCENTRATE ON THE DANTIAN

The lower dantian is our primary source of power. It is our physical and energetic center of gravity. But its formation is not something realized overnight. How can one concentrate on the dantian when this center has not yet been created? Until energy has reached our abdomen we cannot start to create our dantian.

To prepare to form the dantian one begins by relaxing the abdomen and keeping the attention in that area. We can assist this process by keeping our attention here not just in practice, but at all times, in all conditions.

5. ROUND THE SHOULDERS

If your shoulders lost their roundness twenty years ago maybe now they are square! What is natural now is square shoulders, so to make square shoulders round will require a masochistic effort.

The purpose of keeping the shoulders 'soft', is to open and connected the vessels of the shoulders. This goal is common to all the developmental stages, opening – filling – connecting. If we can open the body, we can create the vessels; if we can create the vessels we can improve the body; if we can improve the energy of the body we can develop the vessels. (If we do this nine times, we create an immortal body. But this is an alchemical concept we might discuss in a later book of this series.)

6. GROWING THE ROOTS

It is said that 'rooting' relies on sending the body's energy into the ground, below the soles of the feet. It is said that the feet conduct stability from the floor, up through the knees and hips, and in conjunction with the lower dantian form an agile yet stable posture. But how does one accomplish such a magical feat of the feet? Is it just years of maintaining the correct mechanical alignment of the body? How can we create stability if our body, mind and energy have no stability?

The purpose of a rooted posture is to keep your equilibrium and balance; to have a firm foundation from which to push and to maintain your structural integrity when reaching, connecting or following. Reaching, connecting and following are the roots of Pushing Hands; when these abilities increase you can fill yourself with energy and when you can fill yourself with energy you will understand and apply these principles as they should be.

Ok, but how do we arrive at this place? Rooting occurs of itself, if the principles we are discussing are applied with patience and discipline. If the body has discipline then it will learn to rely on sequence and rhythm, and in time will change. When you can feel that your body is changing you know Jing energy is working. Jing energy has result, but no feeling. If your body feels strong this is the rough energy of Qi. If you body feels empty, but the power that your intention releases has great effect, this is Jing. One thing is sure, there will be no doubt in the practitioner's mind (or body) when they achieve the ability to root.

The head is a vessel in which you must organize the circulation of energy so that it reaches the brain during practice. The center of the brain, Niwang Gong, needs to be filled with energy. If this is achieved, concentration will be improved, resulting in an increase of internal force.

7. HEAD: NECK – EYES – EARS – MOUTH – TONGUE

Keeping control of the head is therefore very important. The head helps to keep the body gathered; it is one of the four cardinal points which must be engaged in the process of constructing the body. The others are feet, spine and chest.

When we can control the head, we can control the eyes, ears, nose and mouth. They are also part of developing concentration. The nose controls breathing, the mouth controls saliva, the eyes control vision and the ears control sound. The wrong use of these organs is a loss of energy. We must learn to develop the ability to remain undistracted by sights and sounds; to keep the breathing calm and to utilize our saliva which becomes impregnated with essence from the brain.

If the alignment of the head, neck and gaze is not correct it disturbs the entire structure and compromises the ability to move without losing the center. The correct attitude of the head is achieved by a gently suspension from above while tucking the chin in slightly. Because at the base the coccyx is tucked, the spine is thus elongated. These opposing tensions open up the vertebrae. When the head is correct, the eyes, ears, nose and mouth will be unobstructed from crown to Bai

Hui (lowest point of the torso). These senses are important in developing our concentration.

Neck

The neck is the connection between head and body and as the circulation of energy only functions properly when the whole body is gathered and connected we can appreciate that if we lose control of the neck we lose control of the connection between head and body. To keep the neck aligned, the practitioner should keep the back of the neck straight and the front of the neck relaxed. In this way saliva can be swallowed to the dantian. Saliva produced during practice is a nourishing substance whose essence can be absorbed by the dantian, and it can facilitate breathing.

Eyes

The eyes connect the body with space. If the body moves forward the eyes must feel this direction. This does not mean that the eyes or head must be turned in the direction of movement. It is that the concentration must be in the direction of movement. Maintaining this sense of concentration through the eyes develops the ability to be aware of the complete space around you, in front and behind.

If the vision is not controlled, concentration is lost, if concentration is lost the feeling of the body is lost, and if the feeling of the body is lost you will not be able to develop the skill of Tui Shou.

The hands, eyes, body, and steps are considered to be the four basic points to observe during practice. It is said that the eyes reveal the mind (windows of the soul), and that to know the mind of the opponent, observe their eyes. So, if the eyes reveal one's internal condition and by doing so give the opponent an advantage, it would be best to develop the internal conditions to neutralize such advantage by turning your own gaze inwards.

Teach the dantian to perceive the significance of what the eyes capture. There is no need for the eyes to 'look', they do that anyway, so the energy of looking should be lowered from the head to the abdomen so that what and how you see is coordinated by the lower dantian. This implies, unfortunately, that until you create the lower cinnabar field you do not really have vision. Hungry, wandering eyes drain the body as surely as an uncontrolled tongue.

Tongue

The tip of the tongue lightly touches the roof of the mouth. This maintains the circuitry of the macrocosmic orbit and helps to produce the saliva or 'clear spring', (said by Daoists to be an elixir associated with longevity). There are three 'ding'. The tip of the tongue touching the hard palate, the attitude of the head and fingers (stretched). From another angle the person suffering from 'motor mouth' also depletes their own energy and that of their captive audience. Experiment with this, look at looking, listen to listening, feel how your body and energy respond in different social situations and you will soon learn how to conserve yourself and move away from negative influences that surround you.

The Harmonies

Harmony is an essence you discover in practice. It relates us back to nature. One who has acquired three harmonies resides in state of naturalness – the very state that Laozi deemed as appropriate for humanity to live in. It is not possible to wish for harmony. To have harmony, your body, mind and energy must change. Although it is somewhat contradictory to the whole idea of harmony often associated with 'peace' and 'calmness', achieving harmony is a hard and gradual work rather than an outcome of some stage.

ENERGY
has body and mind
MIND
has energy and body
BODY

ELBOWS WITH KNEES – SHOULDERS WITH HIPS – FEET WITH HANDS

These are the principle 'connections' which must be formed or created. They create particular changes in the body that eventually lead to achieving harmony throughout the whole body.

Viewed geometrically the body has a top and bottom, left and right sides, a front and a back plus diagonal alignments such as any you care to name, left foot with right hand, or right shoulder with left hip or left toes and right heel. All these opposing and adjacent geometries need to be incorporated into the mind of posture and movement. We can be conscious of these connections during practice so that for example, when the weight is on the right leg, the left leg continues to be engaged. Even though we call it the empty or yin leg it's still a vital part of the structural foundation and this applies to any posture; the whole body is engaged.

EXTERNAL HARMONIES

ELBOWS WITH KNEES

SHOULDERS WITH HIPS

FEET WITH HANDS

**INTERNAL
HARMONIES**

YI
MIND

QI
ENERGY

LI
SPIRIT

YI

From the perspective of harmony, Yi is the connection between Knowledge and Intent.

In Pushing Hands, intellectual knowledge is nothing without body knowledge. We train our energy and body to become natural, i.e. there is no conscious or mental control of movement, the body knows what to do and responds intuitively, by-passing the intervention and obstruction of mind. Of course, mind must be involved in the training that brings us to that place.

QI

From the perspective of harmony, Qi is the connection between Energy and Breath.

Qi is a tool. The natural rhythm of our breathing allows energy to circulate normally. It is the connection between inside and outside. Qi must reach our lower cinnabar field, therefore the breath must reach our lower abdomen. There are alchemical aspects to breath, such as internal breathing and reverse breathing, but they are energetic concepts. Here we are talking, about the physical process, the natural process and rhythm of breathing.

LI

The 'soul' has two parts, Bo souls and Hun souls. Bo souls are the places in your body where a type of energy that can destroy you, inhabits. Hun souls are composed of the three kinds of energy which created us. When we develop our energy it is Hun souls we are creating. Hun souls are the part of us that continues after physical death. Po souls die with the body (having been the agent of death). The cause of death in all cases is the total depletion of energy.

Perhaps this also helps to illustrate the point we make again and again, the victor in Pushing Hands is the one who conquers the enemy within.

The Nine Keys Of Movement

The nine keys are the means to develop the energy you need for growth. You increase your internal pressure when you work with these nine points. Pressure is like soil lying on top of a seed; the seed needs to feel this pressure because it creates a kind of impulse to shoot when the conditions for germination are right.

These nine keys relate to movement, and differ from the postural principles discussed earlier which can be developed in static postures. Movements are important because the shape of movement is like a knot and this mirrors how energy is stored in the body. It forms itself into knots which give it stability and durability so that it is not easily lost. Each key is a knot which helps create not only the pathway for energy but the ability to gather it. To be able to gather energy as we have said many times already is fundamentally important and is most important to your health and to the mastery of Pushing Hands.

People who practice Taiji are often only working with a fairly rough quality of energy and cannot classify the different energetic essences because they have no training with the keys of movement. It's like the handle of the door; whether you like it or not, unless you turn the handle (nine keys) you cannot enter the next level (progress). For example, you can know to 'tuck the coccyx', but this isn't enough; you must know how you can improve your body to make this happen. When we say 'stretch the spine' we send more energy to the coccyx which creates the potential to tuck the coccyx; we must train ourselves to keep energy in this place in order to tuck the coccyx. Likewise we talk about 'lift the crown' but, until we manage to create energy circulation in the neck, you will not keep the crown lifted – it's just not possible. Regardless of how well you comprehend the significance of these keys now, the most important key to all of them is the strength of your intention. All keys have one key – 'remember about the keys'.

The feet must feel each other. This means we keep some concentration on the position and angle of the feet. This angle is between 30 and 60 degrees. In this configuration it is possible for energy to reach the dantian naturally and to flow from the dantian to the root of the feet. The root of the feet, Yong Quan, is the energetic vessel in the middle of the foot, just behind the ball of the foot. It is the junction where the yin and yang meridians of the legs cross over.

THE NINE KEYS OF MOVEMENT

1. Control the Feet
2. Control the Knees
3. Control the Coccyx
4. Control the Lower back
5. Control the Spine
6. Control the Shoulders
7. Control the Elbows
8. Control the Palms
9. Control the Eyes

FEET

KNEES   The knee connects the foot with the hip and therefore controls the spiral of energy in the leg, with the significance that when working properly the speed and force of energy in the leg can be effective. Without this connection energy cannot travel from foot to dantian and vice-versa. We have previously referred to the knees as energetic vessels but in this case we are talking about them as connectors. These are two different functions of the knees. From the perspective of vessels we are talking about the creation of energy and from the connector perspective we are talking about connecting energy.

COCCYX / HIPS   From the perspective of movement we understand that the position of the coccyx and hips organizes or controls the work of the crucible. This is very important, especially in movement, because it controls the area between the legs (crotch) and it controls the flow of energy through the lower center. So, if you lose the hips you lose more than the hips; you lose the possibility to improve your energy!

Knowing about this doesn't mean you can do it and to understand this 'key' you must understand these vessels (coccyx / hips) from the perspective of posture. Until the vessels are open and energy is circulating in them it is very difficult to use them correctly.

LOWER BACK   The main thing to understand regarding movement is the importance of improving the waist. If we can control the body's structure we will be able to utilize all our available energy. If we can control the waist area, the lower back will support and control the front of the body, the abdomen. Successful work with this area depends on the circulation of energy in the waist. The reason we prepare and control this area is because the waist is the junction where multiple body channels intersect. The waist intertwines these energies, enriching the dantian, from where energy is drawn into the microcosmic orbit. Creation of energy is a relatively simple procedure; intertwining it is a skill; achieving energy circulation is an art.

The main point to keep in mind is that the spine is the road for yang energy. We must promote the rise of yang energy, upwards. When you hear the teacher say 'listen behind' he is telling you to listen to the spine. If we can keep the spine, we can keep the energy in the back. Energy has a natural tendency to go forward and when it does, we lose control of the back, hence control of the spine, hence Yang energy cannot rise.

The spine gives us the possibility to understand the whole body, to control the whole body and to operate the whole body. The first part of the work with the spine is to connect upper and lower; this allows us to feel the vertical axis.

SPINE

Slightly softened shoulders ensure that the shoulder joint is not blocking the flow of energy from the middle cinnabar field through to the vessels of elbows and palms. The flow of force from feet to the fingers relies on one's structural integrity. The body must feel and act as one. If the shoulder is out, probably so is the hip. If the hip is out, how can the foot connect to it? If the hip and foot aren't connected, how can the shoulder feel the foot? The legs support the spine, the spine supports the waist, the waist supports the chest, and the chest supports the shoulders. Keep in mind then that while we talk of each part in isolation, they are not so.

SHOULDERS

The elbow controls the rhythm of the hand. The vessel of the elbow must be filled up so that energy can circulate in this zone. Only then can the elbows control the movements of the hand and consequently of the whole body. If the hand can't feel rhythm you may lose energy, because energy cannot reach the palm. To ensure the vessel of the elbows can fill with energy and control the palm, it should 'sink' and turn in slightly toward the body rather than be raised or turned out.

ELBOWS

The key of palms and feet is in the art of gathering the legs and arms. During movement the legs and arms must keep the form. It is the form you must try to keep as a new student of the internal arts. Eventually this will turn the body into a pump that can control energy. But because in the beginning you work at relaxing the body, your legs and arms will not yet have form; they are only organizing the conditions for the form, which the centers of the palms and feet help to organize. All leg meridians connect in the center of the feet, as do the meridians of the arms connect in the center of the palms.

PALMS AND FEET

The eyes must listen. You do not need to 'look' directly at things, the eyes are doing that for you anyway, so the energy of eyes must feel the situation. The eyes must not disturb the body by taking your attention away from the body. When your gaze becomes fixed on something happening outside, the listening inside stops and in this moment you lose control of the body.

EYES

The Thirteen Principles

ONE
Connection and
correspondence

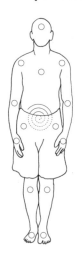

COMMENTARY ON THE FIRST PRINCIPLE

For the practitioner of internal alchemy the body reflects the forms of both the macrocosmos and microcosmos. Wu Ji corresponds to the center, which is physically placed in the navel region, energetically placed within the center of gravity, and spiritually placed within the heart. This center is connected to the energies of the Prenatal and Postnatal Heavens. The body corresponds to the law of duality. There is no top without a bottom, no front without a back, no right side without a left side. One part retreats, while the other part advances. The expression of the yin-yang interaction is the main spiritual feature of most internal martial arts. To connect and to consciously embody these qualities is the accomplishment of one that masters the technique, then this state is found within the practice. It is impossible to master the internal arts without uniting the external with the internal.

We live in a three-dimensional space and our internal and external organs are affected by opposing forces. These forces are working in eight directions with a particular intensity. The axis of the spiritual force corresponds to the vertical path, it is symbolized by Heaven and it relies on the heart-conscious spirit, Shen; the axis of the physical force corresponds to the horizontal path, it relies on the bones and ligaments, Jing and Qi. The axis of the human force corresponds to the middle path, and it relies on the form Jing and Qi, and follows the spirit Shen.

All the axes are in harmony with each other. The correspondence between the organs and the various parts of the body refers to following the three correspondences. The feet are symbolized by Earth and correspond to the shoulders, but also are in accordance with the palms. The palms correspond to the hips, but also are in accordance with the feet. The knees and elbows form the axis for all connections.

The main idea of this principle is the necessity for the concentration of one's consciousness, and then the coordination of the movements, the positions of the body and one's feelings. In this way it is possible to bind the energies harmoniously. Even if these links are felt by the practitioner, they should be enforced by means of concentration. An example of a link would be the right foot and the left palm. It is important not only to link them on the periphery, but also through the center. Then the link not only structures the movement itself, but also creates the ingredients for the alchemical process. In this way the process of compression occurs, which then transforms to expansion. It is necessary to bind all the organs and joints of the body with the center of gravity. This binding can be called the sinking of the Qi to the dantian.

COMMENTARY ON THE SECOND PRINCIPLE

After enforcing the center and the foundation, and the observation of the transformations, the possibility to expand the sphere of the energies' motions will appear. This expanding happens through the stretching and lifting of the sphere. The outlines of the form and the center have equal possibilities for participation in the internal process. They do not exist without each other. There is a motion from the center to the periphery, as there is the motion from the periphery to the center.

TWO
The connection of the center and the foundation

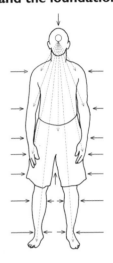

BODY STANCE

In Chinese martial arts the abdomen fills with the breath rather than the upper chest. But this principle regards breath as a movement of energy guided by your attention and should not be thought of simply as the passage of air in the lungs.

THREE
Controlled breathing

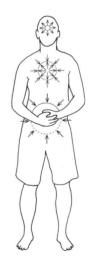

COMMENTARY ON THE THIRD PRINCIPLE

Breathing in the internal practice binds the internal with the external. The function of the breath is the *connection* of the moving energy with the held energy.

The connection can be established on inhalation or exhalation. It does not matter which one is used, but it does matter if there is a connection or not. The connection should not be tightly bound with the physiological inhalation and exhalation.

The second concept is *expansion of the breath* outside of the physiological sphere. The breath should be tuned to the work of the brain and the senses. It becomes not only a nourishing system but also an organizing system. This type of breathing helps the energy to penetrate into the blood vessels and joints of the body.

The third concept is *penetration*. The breath should penetrate into all parts of the body. Then the body becomes a unified breathing form which should then be centralized.

The fourth concept is *centralization*. It implies one source of breathing which binds yin and yang energies into one, thus defining one rhythm.

The fifth concept is *direction*. This type of breathing doesn't have a beginning or an end, but rather has a direction which is necessary for cultivating the internal power.

After the above mentioned principles have been achieved in the given order, the cinnabar breath can be formed. The cinnabar breath is necessary for the fusion of the alchemical ingredients. To hold the breathing in the cinnabar field, the conditions for the penetration of the breath into the cinnabar field should first be created.

FOUR
The controlled groin

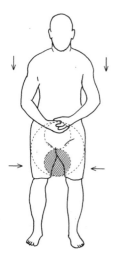

BODY STANCE

Tuck the buttocks, pull in slightly the anus, prostate or womb.

COMMENTARY ON THE FOURTH PRINCIPLE

The groin is the region where the energetic structure can be built. This energetic structure will serve as the foundation for the center of gravity. It will store and hold the energy, strengthening the center of gravity and managing the outburst of energy.

Tuck the buttocks and pull in the anus slightly. For men the prostate gland should also be pulled in. For women the womb likewise should be pulled in slightly. Control of the groin determines whether or not the energy will circulate from the top to the bottom of the body correctly. Failure to control this region could adversely affect the womb, kidneys and prostate gland, as well as causing hemorrhoids.

BODY STANCE

The very tip of the coccyx is tucked under so that one feels a slight pressure on the sacrum. The spine is aligned, vertical and gently extended due to the application of this and the previous principle.

COMMENTARY ON THE FIFTH PRINCIPLE

The coccyx connects the legs with the spine. If the coccyx is not tucked, then the force will be dissipated and the movements will not be coordinated. If the coccyx is tucked then the energy, which moves along the Du Mai meridian, will gather in the center of the stomach and will nourish the cinnabar field.

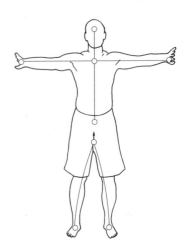

FIVE
The tucked coccyx

BODY STANCE

When any rotation of the body occurs in this practice, the impulse to move and the movement itself is made with the waist. The waist rotates in the vertical axis independently of the hips. This distinction is very important, as the waist is frequently used in these exercises and you will not achieve the desired results if the waist is not properly engaged.

COMMENTARY ON THE SIXTH PRINCIPLE

The waist controls all changes in the position of the body. It connects the bottom of the body with the top. Therefore, it controls virtually all changes in the body. The waist fulfills the function of 'binding' and 'churning'. The binding function is important for the coordination in motion, and the churning function is related to the alchemical transformation, when the energy circulates in the waist meridian. This energy has to be gathered in one of the structures of the lower cinnabar field.

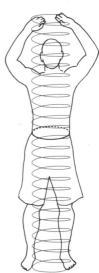

SIX
Loosen the waist

Structures of the lower cinnabar field

SOURCE OF BREATHING
abdomen (men)
solar plexus (women)
SOURCE OF ENERGY
between the kidneys
SOURCE OF SPIRIT
in the liver
SOURCE OF HUN SOULS
in the spleen
SOURCE OF CINNABAR
in the abdomen

The Fajing or outburst of energy also depends on the way the waist works. Every person has a directional rotation which is effortless and natural to him. Usually it is a clockwise rotation. If the energy is developed properly there is no need for effort to turn to the right. The art of managing the waist consists of: falling to the energies of Earth and Heaven; the gathering of the energetic substance in the lower cinnabar field; and the redistribution and bursting out of energy to the necessary point. The main ability involved is to twist the opposite currents of energy.

SEVEN
The hollow chest

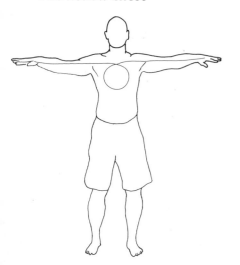

BODY STANCE
The chest should be slightly concave and 'empty'.

COMMENTARY ON THE SEVENTH PRINCIPLE
This principle encourages the openness of the Tian Zhong center. This center manages the yin energy of the middle cinnabar field in men and the yang energies in women. A concave chest also helps to control the spiral rotation and migration of energy.

BODY STANCE

The spinal column is held in light extension. Although the back is vertical, the shoulders are gently rounded.

COMMENTARY ON THE EIGHTH PRINCIPLE

This principle leads to the development and control of yang energy The rounded back is also the basis for the motion and cultivation of energy. This energy moves in a spiral fashion to activate the internal organs. With this principle we develop two qualities of energy: a creating and a gathering energy. The creating energy moves upward, and the gathering energy fills the joints.

The joints determine the movements of the human body. The preparation of the joints will establish the quality of the energy accumulated within them. The synovial fluid is enriched by consciously guiding the energy and holding it in the joints.

Before the bones are formed in the body, the motion of energy is not important because the cartilage performs the function of fluidity in all directions. After the skeletal structure is formed, the loss of limberness follows. To recreate limberness it is necessary to be able to control and guide the energy. The body should be structured so that that energy not only flows freely, but it also accumulates in the joints and energetic vessels.

In alchemical terms this process is concerned with the development of the bone marrow or returning the embryonic qualities to the bones. The nutrient supply for the bones is not the minerals but rather the Jing energy.

Thirty-two pairs of spinal nerves form sixty-four impulses which determine all processes within the body. The practitioner of internal techniques changes, or rather orders, the functioning of the nervous system to transform chaotic energetic processes to a gradual development.

NINE
The loosening of the shoulders and elbows

BODY STANCE

The shoulders remain relaxed, and should not be lifted. The elbows are 'inside' so that the chest can remain 'empty'. The correct shoulder position also assists with the rounded back and hollow chest.

COMMENTARY ON THE NINTH PRINCIPLE

The circulation of energy in the body depends on the position and control of the body. The controlling organs for the body are the shoulders and the elbows. The shoulders allow the energy to sink downward and they connect the arms with the body. If the shoulders are tight, then the circulation of the macrocosmic orbit is broken and the energy will not make a full circle of transformation.

The elbows are the managers of the yang energy. The knees are the managers of the yin energy. The elbows manage the palms and create the foundation for the shoulders and also nourish the heart. The elbows are one of nine energetic vessels that are filled with Heaven energy. They fulfill the function of motion in the process of the transformation of energy. They have a leading role in the yang circle of energy.

TEN
The head suspended from above

BODY STANCE

The spine is in slight extension by a gentle lifting of the vertebrae guided by your attention at the crown of the head at the top and by the tucked coccyx at the bottom. The chin is lightly pulled in, so that the center at the back of the neck is opened.

COMMENTARY ON THE TENTH PRINCIPLE

The head suspended from above helps to hold the energy in the hypothalamus, neck, and palate of the mouth. At the beginning stage it is difficult to feel the motion of energy in the head, and even more so to control it. Basically this work is related to training the brain which is being prepared for further participation in the alchemical transformation process.

The head which is 'suspended from above' means that the spiritual power of Shen is activated. For the practitioner of internal alchemy it means the possibility to transform the energy that forms in the head. It also determines whether or not the practitioner can utilize the energy contained in their saliva; creating in it the necessary essence for the cinnabar field.

FOCUS OF ATTENTION

This principle, as are all the principles, is involved with the constant preoccupation with inner listening. Listening is like vision inside the body and is the ability to feel what is happening in very subtle ways to your body.

This attention is the conscious activity which will guide the energy and create the energetic vessels in preparation for the deeper alchemical work, towards which this practice is directed.

COMMENTARY ON THE ELEVENTH PRINCIPLE

This principle relates to the concept of depth in the practice. As the marrow is something hidden deep inside the body, so the practice is something that is contained inside. Constantly seeking depth in knowledge, the adept tunes himself to the awareness of the unattainable. To penetrate the secret of something, one must know that the important indicator is not the amount of knowledge, but the implied effort of discovery. Every practice is based on the constant effort by which one will accomplish the practice. This constant effort is important for clearing the internal blocks which cannot be dissolved by themselves. The effort is connected with the concentration of consciousness, which clears not only the external and internal organs, but also the consciousness itself.

In alchemical terms we refer to the refining of the marrow and directing the energy to the bones, and the further transformation of that energy as we attempt to recreate the embryonic state of this structure (return to true naturalness).

ELEVEN
Refining
of the marrow

TWELVE
Suspending and rooting

COMMENTARY ON THE TWELFTH PRINCIPLE

In ancient times, it was said that the practices of rooting and suspending in a static form can develop unusual abilities such as levitation and the unmovable stance. The practitioner of Daoist Alchemy and the internal arts such as Pushing Hands has a different purpose; our notion is to apply these qualities or forces within motion.

Rooting can be achieved naturally when the energy is controlled and enforced. To use suspension, however, is more difficult. To manage the lightness, first one should achieve the lightness. One can achieve lightness by working with Jing energy, which takes time to develop. Only then is it possible to manage the flow of energies and therefore manage lightness. The principle of rooting and suspending can be formulated as the ability to manage the top of the body in the upward motion and the bottom of the body in the downward motion. This ability can be achieved by creating different intensities with the dense energies in the body. This is the internal foundation of suspending and rooting.

Note On Feet And Knees

In the thirteen principles just covered, the importance of the feet and knees was not mentioned. The reason for this omission is the fact that the feeling of the knees does not determine the alchemical process. But it is an important condition for the work on all of the principles. Until the centers in the feet and the knees are opened and strengthened, the work on the principles in motion will be impossible. The opening and strengthening of these centers can be accomplished with the practice of special techniques, which are mostly static. In Daoist practice the most efficient systems are those of Dao-Yin and Yijin-jing. It is possible to open these centers in motion also, but it will take more time. The feet are the soil for the internal transformation and the soil should be prepared and nourished before the seed can be planted.

BODY STANCE

Whenever the weight is transferred from leg to leg, the leg on which the weight is placed is termed 'full' (yang) while the other is 'empty' (yin). It is important to keep each leg, energetically, either full or empty.

COMMENTARY ON THE THIRTEENTH PRINCIPLE

This principle relates not only to the distribution of the yin and yang energies, but also the control of yang by yin and yin by yang. This is achieved once the adept is able to hold the consciousness and the energy within the body, while redistributing the intensity of the energy by means of these techniques and one's concentration. The mastering of this principle is also provided by the structuring of the breath and energy.

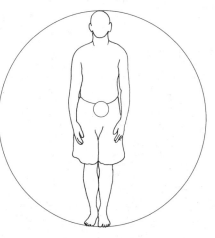

THIRTEEN
Emptiness
and fullness

CHAPTER THREE

Sequence and Rhythm

Sequence and rhythm have important ramifications for our ability to benefit from what we do in practice. We are not just doing something; we must assimilate what we do. The main point of assimilation is to saturate the body and organs with the energy that we generate performing our techniques. In alchemical terms this process follows a logical sequence: first, we 'open' the body; second, we fill the body up; and next, assimilate the gains. So assimilation is the process of savings gains and is a process enhanced if we know how to work intelligently with rhythm.

Assimilation happens as a result of properly organizing the way we practice. We normally practice at a pace that feels natural and comfortable to our level of development and in general, this is fairly slow. The reason it should be slow is that the rhythm of our practice must correlate with the depth of our concentration. To understand how this correlation works we have to tie together the concept of concentration with the concepts of opening, filling-up and assimilating. In the sequence of any practice, we arrive at moments in which the posture can be held for some time, in Taiji Quan we call this 'using the Thirteen Postures'. They are also transition points and these transitions are where we have the opportunity to vary the rhythm of our practice.

In terms of rhythm, we can say a sequence consists of three 'beats': change – stop – assimilation. And, because each posture generates different energetic 'pressures', holding the position for some time allows the vessels to fill up. But the vessels can lose this energy. If we don't know how to assimilate it. Assimilation occurs when we incorporate these three beats of rhythm into our practice, because the key resides in the effort of concentration.

If we were to practice without varying the pace, without transitions or using the Thirteen Postures, it is more than likely we would not sustain a sufficient level of concentration. Mind as well as energy must fill the body.

次序和节奏

To grind wheat we used to use a mill. The mill's large wheel is powered by the movement of water rushing past it. The size the wheel has a relation to the flow of the river and in this way the speed of rotation is optimized for the grinding of the wheat. Too slow and we grind insufficient flour, too fast and the wheat will not be ground properly, so the wheel must have the correct rhythm. Whoever constructs a mill must understand rhythm, for if he was to build a large wheel but have not sufficient water flow, he will not create the ingredients to nurture himself. Therefore one must think about the construction of the mill. In our practice, rhythm creates the structure. We can make wine and in ten years it will reach maturity, but the quality of the wine depends just as much on its preparation in the very early stages as it does on its cellaring. In the making are many processes; some are fast, others take time.

The concept of rhythm has many dimensions and is quite elaborate. We mentioned rhythm in relation to 'pace' and related it to the assimilation of energy during practice. Rhythm can also be viewed on a larger scale in reference to seasons. For thousands of years in Ancient China the importance of seasonal change was noted not only by peasants who followed the calendar in their rural life, but also by alchemists. Seasons determined conditions for particular activities that had to be undertaken in each period. Most importantly, for the farmer to maximize their harvest or for the alchemist to pick the right moment in the celestial cycle for transformation, their activities needed to be in harmony with nature.

To work with the eight energies in harmony with the celestial cycles, we need to transform the energy in our body at the end of each season. In Daoist Alchemical Law the period between seasons is the center; at this point energy reaches its peak and naturally begins to transform. So, in the height of summer we can find the seeds of autumn. The center point is the period between seasons when one cycle finishes and another begins. But 'alchemical' time refers more to time than to seasons and usually refers to the quality and intensity of alchemical work and concentration. Of course this process can be aligned with the yearly seasonal cycles but is not dependant upon them.

A Practice For Understanding Rhythm

The energy of the waist generates two orbits which are a function of the waist meridian. We have two practices which work with these orbits and which help us to understand rhythm and energy because they work with the internal principles of the body. These two orbits and the corresponding practices for working with them are the 'small' and 'large' spirals of the waist.

The waist is an internal orbit which connects upper and lower parts of the body. It must manage three types of connections: front/back, left/right, above/below.

Six sectors of the waist

The waist is divided into six sectors. During the day energy undergoes six transformations because each part is activated differently according to the hour and season. Therefore we can say that the waist has six sources or 'wells'. But, this creates a problem that makes it difficult to work with and activate the waist, because the sensations we are trying to understand are in constant flux. When we work with the waist we must activate one of these six sources in order to circulate more energy in the waist meridian. If this is not a regular practice, only one part in six will be activated and that is the main hindrance to our growth.

If we wish to develop skilfull Pushing Hands we must work at least three times a week with the waist orbits, big and small. It also has implications for the rest of our practice, not just Pushing Hands. Movements cannot be connected if the waist is not activated, with the result that we cannot benefit fully from our practice because we will not gather, keep and save the energy it generates. That is why we are talking about the waist right from the start.

After we understand the principles for constructing the body we must seek to understand 'rhythm'. The source of rhythm lies in the waist.

Small And Large Orbit Exercises

At all times, keep your concentration on the palms (sky and earth), for in this exercise the waist is sustained by the palms. When we activate the waist meridian, energy begins to circulate in a spiral manner.

Fig 3.1

Fig 3.2

Fig 3.3

SMALL SPIRAL OF THE WAIST

1. Concentrate on the waist.
2. Step back with right foot. (Keep weight forward). Left palm supports 'sky'. Right palm is sustained by 'earth'.
3. Turn waist right.
4. Change weight.
5. Change hands. Right palm supports 'sky'. Left palm is supported by 'earth'.
6. Turn left. Change palms again.
7. Change weight (to the front).

Fig 3.4

Fig 3.5

Fig 3.6

LARGE SPIRAL
OF THE WAIST

1. Concentrate on the waist.
2. Step back with right foot. (Keep weight forward).
Right palm supports 'sky'. Left palm is sustained by 'earth'.
3. Turn waist left. Change hands.
4. Change weight.
5. Turn waist right. Change hands.
6. Turn waist left. Change hands.
7. Turn waist right. Change hands.
8. Change weight (to the front).
9. Turn waist left.
10. Feet together. Concentrate on and feel the waist.

Fig 3.7

Fig 3.8

Fig 3.9

Fig 3.10

Fig 3.11

Fig 3.12

Fig 3.13

CHAPTER FOUR
Yin-Yang

In this chapter you will learn about the importance of realizing the Yin-Yang principle as a tool to refine energy. Through refinement we begin by initially separating physical from energetic. Once we get a clearer idea about energetic power as opposed to physical might, we can distinguish between different states of energy, which is the first step towards applying refined energy and channeling the right kind of energy to the right location. Yin-Yang deepens the understanding of rhythm, body construction and concentration by facilitating the refined energy to circulate in the orbit and may be followed by reiteration of these first three formative stages.

In the practice of internal martial arts there are two directions of movement; one direction creates Yin energy, the other Yang. Yang is the energy for growth and change. All modern forms of Taiji Quan, for example, work with Yang energy.

The closest translation from Chinese, and for that matter, the best interpretation of Yin-Yang is the concept of duality. Duality can mean a range of things and describes, for example, opposing forces. The graphical manifestation of Yin-Yang is the well known symbol used in just about in everything related to energy. And not without a reason – the concept is so profoundly important that our existence would be impossible without it.

Let's look at them separately. Yang is function of movement; Yin is function of calmness. Yang relates to the vertical axis; Yin to the horizontal axis. 'When Dragon meets Tiger' – this is the interaction between Yin and Yang. Coupling properties in movement – connections between back and front, top and bottom, left and right – are all described by Yin and Yang.

Whichever object or action you look at it always finds harmony by matching or merging with its opposite. Therefore, finding a harmonious state of interaction of the two

is seen as a remedy in illness and key to balancing the energy. On a deeper level when yin and yang are 'melted' together in union (balanced), the form is said to be in harmony. When the form is in harmony, it is pure, as when reaching a state of the Ultimate. Purity of the form is a requirement for the distribution of energy into the three dantians. When yin and yang find themselves in the body's cauldrons, Dragon and Tiger play in the stirring river, Sun and Moon have reflections in each other and man and wife seclude themselves in the bedchamber.

Golden Crow and Jade Hare symbolize the essence of yin and yang. Crow is the guardian of Heaven, Hare is the guardian of the Earth; when crow flies down to Earth and Hare jumps up to Heavens, it is said that channels are open and energy can circulate from head to the lower dantian (or that microcosmic orbit is circulating).

This is a rather philosophical interpretation of Yin-Yang principle and it has been known to the West in number of forms and adapted as a symbol of spirituality worldwide. For Pushing Hands practice purposes we are concerned with practical applications of this highly alchemical concept.

Realizing the yin-yang principle is complemented by the ability of the practitioner to feel the nature of energetic flows in the body, which is very important for establishing circulation. Refining and separating various qualities of energy, or rather, understanding that energy has three levels to it, is yet another skill which is introduced by yin-yang.

Nothing is more than a feature or quality of energy, rather than energy itself. And all descriptions lead to that exercise because it helps to organize practice, which in turn helps realize the interaction between yin and yang.

To understand the concept yin-yang, all movement must be constructed from the lower dantian. During movement this center is called the 'Minor sphere'. Even if you cannot feel the Minor sphere you must continue to focus your attention on the abdomen and struggle to realize its significance.

At first it's like a cocoon from your center to Lao Gong and then from Lao Gong to center. Doing the correct movement is less important than the connections you can make and the transitions between the movements. Energy during movements must intertwine with itself in the manner of a loom joining threads together.

**Lao Gong
center**

Fig 4.1 Fig 4.2 Fig 4.3

Fig 4.4 Fig 4.5 Fig 4.6

CAPTURING YIN-YANG

First organize the Minor sphere.
Start to unwind the Minor sphere.
Start to create Yang energy.
Do this until you reach Major Yang.
Untwist until you reach Major Yang.
Wind until you reach Major Yin.

This intertwining will be difficult to achieve without the notion of rhythm as a consistent pattern which can produce consistent results (like threads of equal thickness during looming). It's another kind of practice where the accuracy of the movements is important. In this practice the important consideration in the movement is yin/yang, open/close, front/back. If the body is not ready it's difficult to do, but it is necessary to understand the different kinds of work to prepare yourself for Pushing Hands.

CHAPTER FIVE
Listening

> 'My spirit allows me to know what is coming.
> My wisdom allows me to hide the attack.'
> Chen Xin

Listening is a conventional concept known well in Taiji and other martial arts. Depending on the level of the practitioner we are concerned with two applications of listening.

The first application is relevant to every practitioner but especially so for beginners. This refers to listening to yourself, your energy and your reaction. At this stage the practitioner recaps what has been achieved so far and has the capacity to observe the mistakes and shortcomings that reveal themselves. This can be done either independently as a meditative exercise or with a partner.

Working with a partner for the same purpose (realizing one's shortcomings) is the second application of listening. Here the practitioner is required not only to listen to oneself but also to one's partner. Attention to detail must be extended beyond simply watching out for wrong movements and unnecessary energy outbursts. Body, energy and spirit must work coherently together to benefit to the fullest extent from this interaction with the partner's force. And, although the focus is still on oneself, one can no longer ignore the power coming from the 'external environment'.

In Pushing Hands we equate the skill of internal listening with a quality of energy and this energy is called 'listening' Jing. To 'hear' the very subtle, internal movements of our opponent and thus anticipate their next move requires a very high degree of sensitivity, and it is this sensitivity that allows us to respond intuitively and instantly in any situation. To respond intuitively means we must do away with preconceived strategies, because how can we act originally if we already have a plan of action? To be without preconceived strategies

Three qualities of listening:
LISTENING QI
The art of feeling
LISTENING JING
Finding the root of force
LISTENING SHEN
The art of filling up

is to be in a state of emptiness or naturalness. To be empty is to carry no obstruction to perception. The state of emptiness is one of readiness, of patience, of inner stillness and alertness made possible by the our body's awareness of its own energy field. If we can feel our own energy field we can feel any force that enters into it. This is the essence of listening; awaking our own perception of our self in order to extend that sensitivity to what is outside the body.

The essence of our treatise is to introduce you to the principles of Daoist Alchemy that underlie the system of Pushing Hands, whereby you may defeat your own ignorance and disease. That you can overcome an opponent is no more than a reflection of your progress toward the state of naturalness that ensues from the practice of this art.

In Pushing Hands, 'listening' Jing is the most important energy to develop. But without Qi it is not possible to create Jing. If we can create the listening spiral (energy during listening has a spiraling movement) we will achieve the state of listening Jing.

Listening is the art of connecting; it allows us to find the right effort for any situation. If we listen to music, we listen not just to the lyrics but also to the 'effort' that created those words. When we see the body, we must see what's inside the body; what is filling the body. In relation to listening, it means to find the point where movement is starting from, or the root of each movement.

In the art of listening if we wish to connect something we need to have two points and something to connect these two points – a third element. With listening we are preparing the conditions to move energy and for this we need to know where the energy will move, from where to where (the two points), and create a situation in order to connect them – the third element. This third element can be inside or outside the body; it can be anything that helps us to connect the two points. For example, the dantian acts like a third element when energy of different body parts is connected. The dantian intertwines the two flows of energy (creating the energetic 'knot'). Without the third element, two points would be related but not necessarily connected. Connection yields enrichment of the third point which extracts the alchemical ingredients from it and yields the assimilation of energy.

To develop listening we use six axes or efforts – right/left, up/down, front/back. These six listening efforts create our 'listening spiral' (the third element). The following exercise creates this 'listening spiral'. The spiral is a play between two spirals with opposing rotations, a Yin and Yang spiral. If you take a wet towel and twist it to eject the water, both hands are making a spiral, but the right hand is working in the opposite direction to the left. This is the yin-yang spiral. At the same time we are creating the effort to wring the water out; this is the third element we referred to above. The Yin-Yang effort is what creates the listening spiral.

When you do this exercise try to feel that the palms are like opposite ends of the towel you are wringing out. If you don't really understand the concept behind this exercise, remember two things: your hands are a Yin/Yang axis and you change this axis. Changing the two ends of the axis, or these two points, is like creating the listening spiral. This exercise involves six efforts that create the third element.

Fig 5.1   Fig 5.2   Fig 5.3

Fig 5.4   Fig 5.5   Fig 5.6

CHAPTER SIX

Long and Short Energy

'The best use of theory is in better practice'.

'Long' and 'short' energy are two types of energy we create in different exercises to 'construct' the body. Our main goal with these two energies is to learn the 'Art of Gathering' the body. In our work with long energy the first thing we try to achieve is to untwist our energy. Energy does not move linearly, it moves in a spiral, so when we work with long and short energy we are working to open this spiral and gather energy. In this chapter you will understand the significance and purpose of 'long' and 'short' energy and learn two exercises for developing it. 'Minor Yang' is energy which activates movements over a short distance; it is a minor movement which packs a lot of power. Short energy can be applied by just one part of the body. Short energy is easier to feel when the body assumes a 'gathered' posture, such as when preparing to strike or push. Vertical movements use short energy. Short energy is developed when Minor Yang is working.

'Long' energy is easier to feel when the body is in open postures (when Major Yang is working). Both long and short energy can be present in any posture, and in fact the two energies do not operate in isolation, one relies on the other, but it will be easier if you try to feel it under these conditions just described. When the whole body is engaged in movement this is the application of long energy. When movement is horizontal we are using long energy.

长
精
短
精

Long energy requires much more time and effort to develop than short energy, but, on the other hand, short energy requires absolute control over the minor zone of its operation. Both long and short energy can be used in all kinds of movements. In the beginning the body moves energy but at later stages energy moves the body. When the body moves energy, we rely on short energy, but when energy moves the body, we rely on long energy.

To develop short energy we have some exercises with a Taiji ball. The ball helps us to concentrate on the internal principles and in doing so short energy is created because the movements of the sequence are not large, open actions, they are slow and contained close to the body. Our concentration is inside the body.

To develop long energy we can use the Taiji stick. The movements of this sequence make the stance of the body much more open so that we must connect our body with the end of the stick, meaning that our concentration is outside the body.

The exercise we depict in the following images may be practiced in two ways. If you are a new student, hold each posture for some time to gather your body. For more advanced practitioners the sequence can be used both as a series of static postures and as a continuous movement without breaks between the transitions.

Exercises For Working with Short Energy

| Fig 6.1 | Fig 6.2 | Fig 6.3 | Fig 6.4 |

Fig 6.5 Fig 6.6 Fig6.7 Fig 6.8 Fig 6.9

Fig 6.10 Fig 6.11 Fig 6.12 Fig 6.13 Fig 6.14

Fig 6.15 Fig 6.16 Fig 6.17 Fig 6.18 Fig 6.19

Exercises For Working with Long Energy

Fig 6.20

Fig 6.21

Fig 6.22

Fig 6.23

Fig 6.24

Fig 6.25

Fig 6.26

Fig 6.27

Fig 6.28

Fig 6.29

Fig 6.30

Fig 6.31

Fig 6.32

Fig 6.33

Fig 6.34

CHAPTER SEVEN

Developing Forces An and Ji

An and Ji are the main forces underlying the skills of Pushing Hands. They are the basis of understanding the body through constructing one's energy. They teach us how to twist and untwist, to open and close and how to work with what is outside and inside the body.

提高按劲和挤劲

Eight Forces Of An

Force Li is the heart of all the forces, it teaches to one to listen, to cooperate and to understand how the energy is shown. And though the coordination of all vessels is important for all forces, it is shown most clearly in the movements of body Li. It is Li force which harmoniously connects the movement of long and short energies. The source of the short energy is the horizontal field; the source of long energy is the vertical field. The connection of these fields allows Li force, or fire, to be shown. Maintaining the horizontal field in a body occurs by means of knees, hips, shoulders and elbows, as well as feet and hands. Maintaining the vertical field occurs through centers of Hui Yin, Ba Hui and Yun Quan.

Li force clearly shows not only the connectedness of the fields and vessels, but also the circulation of the alchemical orbits. In the display of this force the second cinnabar field receives the basic development. If an adept achieves comprehension of this force, he wins over Bo souls. In this case Bo souls cannot render their destroying influence and cannot neutralize the energy body, or harm the physical one as well. Hence a direct road for cultivating of Shen is open.

Developing this force we strengthen our perception and interrelation of the microcosmos with the macrocosmos. Besides, this force has an important quality; it feeds the middle cinnabar field. We mean the circulation of the chest orbit, which is projected from the waist orbit.

To let this force be shown one needs a changed physical body and it means that the frame of the body must be built according to alchemical laws, which happens when Li force is located in the lower cinnabar field and Ji force in the middle cinnabar field. Naturally, these forces in the human body are located vice versa, and the center of these energy transformations appears to be the breast instead of the abdomen. In the transformed body the center of energy transformations moves to the abdomen. If the body is not ready for such realization, the force should be used for transformation of the body instead of realization of the quality. It depends on the practitioner.

A strike, which symbolizes the meaning of Li force, does not mean that someone should be pushed. First of all it means a skill to transform and to find the connection, which shows the qualities of a strike. Each force is already a certain result, and this result should manifest itself. Only the demonstrated result gives true comprehension of the force, and lets one understand what it is necessary for and in what it should result. The result, which an adept must achieve, should let him coordinate the internal sphere with the external sphere. Li force permits the harmonious combination of the horizontal and vertical axes of the energy matrix. In applying this force, the body should receive an internal satisfaction; the centripetal movement of energy should be connected with its centrifugal characteristic. For this purpose it is necessary to achieve a connection of Lao Gong with Yong Quan, or the center of a palm with the center of a foot. If an adept loses this connection or if it is not felt, they fail to achieve realization of the force. In developing Li force we develop the internal fire, in developing the internal fire we get an opportunity to extract cinnabar, and thus to strengthen our body.

The basis of Ji Ji force is made by the external display of Li force. The force presents harmony of both Li force and Ji force and the development of this force is connected with hearing of the center Dantian. During the process of realization of the force an adept must achieve accumulation in Dantian and its settling. Mastering the force it is necessary to achieve linkage of a movement when there is one movement in another. Then it is possible to say that Li and Ji get linked and Ji Ji force finds its realization. Li is the basic force here; it means that the movement should occur through a prism of hearing. There is an internal rigidity in a visible external softness. The movement is directed at collecting of Earth and strengthening of Spirit. Due to shaking, which helps to separate the ingredients, all this frames ideal conditions for creation of cinnabar. It is especially necessary keep the abdomen relaxed when performing this force. The opportunity of realization of this force also depends on how well the waist meridian is developed. If it is not developed the work should be directed at it, first of all, and only then it is possible to work at manifesting the force.

Depending on whether the force can be realized or not, it is possible to make a conclusion. While performing the force a practitioner must preserve the form, it must not be lost or distorted. It means to achieve a transforming meaning incorporated in Ji Ji. In spite of an apparent simplicity of the force, it coordinates three vertical axes with themselves – the central axis and two lateral ones – which connect shoulders with hips. The loss of one of the axes does not let the force

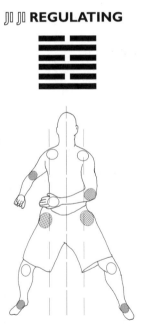

JI JI **REGULATING**

manifest, as the axes help to keep the bottom cinnabar field where all this process takes place.

Working with Ji Ji, it is necessary to concentrate on the gatheredness of hands and on the connection of the centers of hands with the center of the breast. Listening to legs and waist by arms should preserve the basis and force, and they (arms) must be connected with each other during any movement.

We also draw your attention to the fact that at the end of realization of the force there should be a certain compression or pressure in the middle field. As a result, Bo souls get cemented and coordinated which permits their control. The filling of the vessels in the force is regulated: feet are filled, knees are empty, hips are filled, shoulders are empty, elbows are filled, hands are empty.

GE CHANGE

Ge is a withdrawing movement; it relies on the internal force of fire. We can characterize this force thus: the brain absorbs – the body moves – the energy breathes. It has a demonstrable basis; it is a basis of transformation. Heaven and Earth find the new by means of transformation. The transforming force appears to be the practitioner himself; one who not only helps to find the new, but also serves as a basis himself. In spite of insufficient understanding of the movement (and it can be connected with a diagonal component of the force), it has an internal clarity. The internal clarity is always shown when Yin and Yang find correspondence.

The force is realized through passage of the movement along a diagonal, thus connecting Earth with Heaven. In a process of the movement the energy passes through six transformations or six levels of changes. The energy, being transformed in the foot, moves to the knee, being transformed in the knee, moves to the hip, being transformed in the hip, moves to the shoulder, being transformed in the shoulder, moves to the elbow, being transformed in the elbow, moves to the hand. Having achieved a general connection we get a feeling of pleasure.

In Ge force, energy moves similar to a movement which a leopard makes in a jump. We mean the energy which untwists a leopard during his jump. But in a process of landing, a leopard is transformed into a tiger. The tiger here acts as a display of calmness. Thus it points at newly acquired qualities received at the end of a display of Ge force. It is necessary to understand that comprehension of the force cannot be reached at once, but after sets of attempts you are sure to be accompanied by success.

The main thing that the force teaches is that a practitioner should not treat this force carelessly otherwise success will be never achieved. Here the importance of concentration is underlined and it should proceed first of all from the body. Concentration understood by a brain and concentration understood by a body are absolutely different things. Concentration from the position of a brain is a meaning indicating an action and nothing else. Concentration from the position of the body is internal knowledge which becomes demonstrable through its external manifestation. The body can inform the brain about this knowledge, but the brain cannot render any appreciable influence on the body. Therefore, participating in development of a body, the brain should not prevent it being impregnated with force since the force cannot exist outside the body. It is the phenomenon that exists inside and not the aspects that remain outside that we rely on. But in keeping yourself from excessive diligence you may face the danger of expectation that appears to be the opposite of diligence.

MINGYI **TWILIGHT**

Ming Yi force symbolizes the depth of listening or the place from which listening develops and proceeds. The center of listening is the abdomen. Developing our abdomen (lower cinnabar field) we develop listening. A human body acquires another quality of perception not only of itself but also of environmental space. The deeper the body perceives, the more opportunities of realization it has. Thus the body gets a new potential for development of energy, physical and spiritual processes.

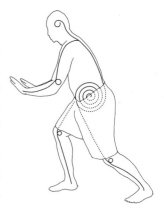

To some extent Ming Yi force, in the process of exerting the force, strengthens itself and thus its transformation is achieved. The movement of Ming Yi force is inertial. The external display of the force is quiet. The effort is directed inside. In the movement of this force yin adds fire to the stove. The basis here is solely the internal fire, as the external sphere is passive. But there can be completeness in the use of this force. Completeness here will mean that the fire fades and hence there will be a loss of the force.

To realize Ming Yi force it is necessary to be ready to face the body's anxiety and uneasiness to understand this force. This anxiety is connected with the fact that the body does not know what is wanted from it. There is an external direction but there is no internal application for this direction. On the one hand there is an opportunity for cultivating the fire; on the other hand there is a danger of its loss.

Here there is a very thin line between opening and closing. Controlling of the force is also complicated by the fact that it is very difficult to apprehend this thin line between external passivity and internal activity. In the force, consciousness and the body seem to be relieved of the process; if they are introduced into it, the force dies and cannot develop. There is a certain contradiction in the movement of this force, as the vectors of the movement of the external and internal spheres move in the opposite directions. If a practitioner manages to avoid the contradiction, then the natural harmony balancing Heaven and Earth is realized. Or in other words, it is possible to keep the monad of rest (to preserve the condition of energy's transforming in the form), dominant in the force. It is not necessary to search for completeness in Ming Yi, so it is easier to understand this force. To understand it means to learn to listen to softness.

TONG REN
COMMUNITY

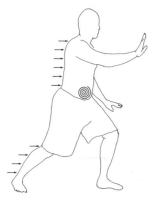

Tong Ren force opens the internal fire. It relies on the readiness of the internal fire for realization and listens to it. Developing this force we develop clarity of movement and we frame an opportunity not only to fill movement, but also to realize it, taking into account the opportunities of the internal sphere.

Tong Ren force helps to find and to remove all blocks which can appear in the way of the movement of energy. Success of Tong Ren's display depends on the skill of connecting listening and force. At the same time it demonstrates the level an adept has achieved. If the energy reaches a finishing point, passing through a spiral of movement, then the body is open for achievements. The movement can be considered completed when the spiral is completely opened. It means that it has a basis, or the beginning, and it has the end – the point where the force is transformed or lost. The skill of listening to the movement of the force is the thing that allows us to transform the energy and not to lose it. A necessary skill to do this is an ability to 'catch' the energy.

Catching energy depends on the rate of listening. The rate of listening determines the rhythm of changes. At first it is necessary to learn simply to listen or, rather, to feel, then it is important to learn to distinguish and identify the sensations, in order to understand their nature. Only then it is possible to learn comprehension of the movement. Without comprehension of the nature that forms the movement it is impossible to understand the movement. And the changes are understood only when the movement is understood, as it is the moment of balancing energy.

But there is a danger which is mitigated by the process of development of this force. It is connected with a loss of a true basis and occurs when an adept develops not an internal basis, but an external one. It can move an adept away from the concept of Tong Ren force. The movement should proceed from the abdomen and be understood by it.

Putting this force into practice it is not necessary to be afraid of doing it the wrong way. It is a force that can be performed incorrectly initially. 'Incorrect' is understood here as the development of the external sphere. In any case if the rate of performing of the movement is not lower than average, the body gets a good shake and opens. It changes the energy's circulation by means of which an additional opening becomes possible and in its turn gives a shake to the energy. It helps to remove blockages of the external sphere.

Jia Ren is a force demonstrating the principles or correct listening to the principles, which are opened as a result of action of the internal fire or as a result of action of the force in the house.

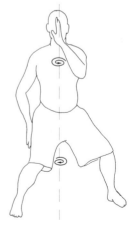

Jia Ren force ascertains the condition of the energy which fills the body. On the one hand there is an internal fire which makes the energy move and even develop; on the other hand an uncontrollable state like wind dispersing or dissipating the energy. Though dispersion occurs inside a vessel, all the same there is a danger of losing energy if a practitioner does not understand its movement and cannot coordinate it. But in order to understand and coordinate it, first one must learn to listen to it. If the body is developed it has a source inside the abdomen (a place where energy is reproduced), which determines development of the internal fire. If the body is not developed the role of the source can be played by any organ which produces Jing energy. More often it is sexual energy or cerebral energy (the energy determined by the vessels of a head). That is, the internal fire is defined by the place which serves a source of this fire. And directions in which this energy can move, i.e. eight directions, determine the filling by energy of the body's vessels from this source.

Naturally, the movement of all eight directions cannot be seized and so we speak about it as the influence of a controlled or uncontrolled wind. A controlled wind implies that energy moves like a spiral which naturally covers all eight directions. When the wind is uncontrollable it means that energy moves in a dissipated manner. So the internal fire directed by the controlled wind makes the essence of the Jia Ren force. That means that energy is constantly in the house.

It is also necessary to understand that the controlled wind can exist only when the source is centered. The centered source is found in the abdomen, in the Supreme Center. In general, all forces can certainly be surveyed only in relation to the Supreme Center. Only in this case it is possible to create a successive chain of Laws described by the hexagrams. Any movement apart from the center when performing this force leads to a formal character of practice, i.e., when the force is manifested only on the level of its conventional-formal meaning. Like the other forces Jia Ren force belongs to the body of listening or An body. Hence an important feature here is a circulation of energy, which actually supports the form of a vessel.

FENG **PROSPERITY**

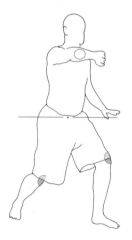

Feng is an application of Li force which strengthens absorption of the force by means of its gathering listening on the horizontal axis. It symbolizes change. Everything that was reached by the fire is shown here in conditions of constancy. In spite of an obvious character of realization of the force it should not have a broken or interrupted character. The more precisely the plane is sustained, the clearer the force is and the brighter its display. This force has the meaning of internal knowledge. It helps one to understand a new acquisition. Listening to the force an adept comprehends the formula, which explains the internal.

In the application of this force it is important to control the processes. As the loss of energy is inevitable, an adept must try to benefit from it. If energy is freed it creates the condition for acquisition of new energy. It means new opportunities for energy transformation and for training of the vessels as their flexibility and elasticity develop. If the vessels are not yet ready to understand this then it is necessary to continue to stretch and to shake them in order to let them acquire knowledge of themselves. All this implies prosperity.

The concept of Bi force includes so much that one can fail to see its true meaning behind a definition of a Shoulder Strike. It is so thin and graceful that it requires a very serious approach.

Shoulders symbolize a vertical component of a vessel. They appear to be a basis for the central axis. It is impossible to make an effort with a shoulder if its connection with the central axis is broken, because the latter is connected with the lower field – a source of power.

The physical body is universal; it has a given orbit of rotation, which is outlined by the lateral vertical axes passing through the centers of shoulders and hips. At the moment of rotation, energy moves from the lateral axes to the central one forming a well-known symbol – Yin-Yang.

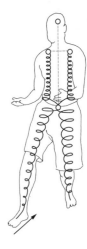

Bi force characterizes connections, which are built by means of these axes. If the connections are built, the body naturally moves in all directions. But in order to achieve it there must be a constant process of filling in every moment of movement. Only in this case the internal fire will be supported.

Bi force has a steady form, as actually do all forces, which includes the meaning of Kao, or Mountain. The loss of the form will result in a loss of an axis and accordingly power. But, nevertheless, it will allow one to support an internal viscosity, toughness, ductility (knots), enabling an adept to strengthen density of this force and to alter it.

A human condition has a given scale of density in relation to which an effort can change. Another important feature of the force is generation of the other force. The form having the internal fire is always ready to change and all eight directions appear to be dependent on it.

Eight Forces Of Ji

Wei is a force which embodies 'listening' the manifestation of this force is uniting. If there is no union there can be no changes, and where there are no changes there cannot be completeness. Wei is a gate which opens our mind to the concept of changes. Changes that occur during practice must be inter-related between each other and at all times controlled and traced by our consciousness. This is one of the main tasks of alchemy because, in order to obtain the internal elixir, the process of change has to be controlled and paid attention to. When we say controlled we especially emphasize the importance of being aware of difficult conditions, for example when you need to select a special time or place or other circumstance in order to complete the alchemical process or stage of alchemical process. This force, as well as all other forces within the sphere Ji, helps us to feel the action in a deeper way.

This force is described by Jing energy which doesn't have a well defined form but has a very well defined manifestation. This force forms a 'cinnabar water'. Once cinnabar water is filled we can say that the alchemical process has a rhythm, but before that can happen you have to feel the alchemical process within your body. Feeling this process is what we call listening; only when you listen can you distinguish the new achievements and separate them from what you have achieved earlier.

Wei teaches us to refine our existence and our practice and understand the connections within the body on a deeper level. We should depart from linear concepts such as right and left and up and down, and look deeper into what defines and what is the reason behind the connection being between upper and lower, between right and left, and so on. In other words, we need completeness which we can then separate into components and then work with them individually, otherwise we are always destined to wander in chaos. Because that is very important, the form has to be developed and worked on until it can be understood as a sphere.

While the form is not complete, it is linear and when the form is linear it cannot be considered a form. Only after the form can be subjected to changes can the transformation process start and then the form is no longer incomplete.

When we combine alchemical changes which occur inside together with their external counterparts which happen as a result of these alchemical changes, this is described by the force Song. When our internal condition doesn't allow for external changes this creates stagnation or, worse, it can create a struggle between the two. The force Song teaches us to find and connect the inconsistencies which may exist between our body and energy and it shows us the right way out of such a difficult situation.

The group of forces which comprise Ji pay particular attention to the internal sphere and through that it refines the manifestation of force Peng (one of the eight forces). At the same time, force Peng, which relates or describes the external sphere, strengthens Ji, the internal sphere. In a way this strengthening of Peng by Ji and Ji by Peng comes out of the struggle between them rather than a complementary effect. This makes it difficult to understand this process, but, at the same time, on the way to understanding it, understanding the relation between the internal and external spheres opens up new ways and possibilities for the practitioner.

Force Song describes the power which is hidden deep down inside. No matter what the external manifestation of this power is, the origin is always inside (internal). This is very important to remember in any movement or action that you do. Whatever repetition that you do externally to refine and to feel the movement is no more than a repeated attempt to get a deeper, more insightful understanding of the internal power, internal force.

If the internal force that is trying to manifest itself externally is not controlled, then it will always be an obstacle and your external efforts, your repetitions in other words, will never succeed. Even though it may seem that you are getting closer and closer to understanding the connection between them, this is only temporary. No matter how far you advance in your external exercises that you do without support of the internal power, sooner or later all your external efforts will be useless. The longer that happens and the longer you ignore the connection between internal and external the greater the danger of the cyclic dependence, the greater the chances of stagnation and the further away you will be getting from understanding the internal part of what you're doing. Ultimately, that completely separates your external movement from the internal reasoning for it and you may fail to feel them ever. This is a very important idea because, similar to any artistic skill, if it doesn't in the end rely on some internal support or internal source of

power sooner or later it will fail or diminish. You can spend a very long time creating the external conditions and external form, but without internal fulfillment it will be impossible to achieve satisfaction from whatever you have created.

Even though your mind might understand this concept clearly and you might agree with it, the true understanding of its depth is impossible without the condition of 'naturalness' – without you achieving a natural state. Therefore before working and attempting to get the force Song to manifest itself, it is important to achieve the natural state.

HUAN
DISPERSION

The concept of Huan describes an action that takes place in a constrained space. If control over the force is maintained at all times it is said that a positive essence is developed from the movement; if you lose control and your force is free to move around then the result of your action will be negative essence. The ability of this force to manifest itself and the ability to work with this force very much depends on the level of development of the form. If the sphere has been previously created then it is easier to feel this force because it moves according to the correct principles. If the sphere is not there then this force will disperse itself.

In addition to external work, this force also features a serious external effort. Both external and internal complement each other when this force manifests itself. The internal is accomplished through the external and the external is complemented by the internal. In reference to this particular force, this idea of mutual complement leads us to a very important alchemical term of interaction: a game between the Green Dragon and White Tiger. It is also referred to as a reaction between lead and mercury. However the important aspect of this event that we must understand is not the interaction itself but rather understanding the reasons behind these interactions. In fact, this understanding can come from the practice of different forces and not only from force Huan. Force Huan prescribes that the interaction between the Green Dragon and the White Tiger is possible under different conditions, but given all these different conditions there is only one foundation these conditions can base themselves on. In other words, this force teaches us that a foundation is required so that an interaction between Green Dragon and White Tiger can occur under conditions of different forces.

It is also important that the form has already been developed enough to be able to comprehend or accept the results of this interaction. The preparedness of the form can be distinguished by the presence of the 'Alchemical Fire'. The Alchemical Fire is controlled by the forces Ji and An. The Alchemical Fire is one which can melt the alchemical ingredients rather than burn them. The Supreme Center can only be created when the alchemical ingredients are melted together and this is called the growth of the 'Yellow Sprout'. Force Huan describes the internal sphere connected or joined with the water element. This is a rather dangerous state of affairs for the alchemical process because water prevents the internal process from developing, which is why the water has to be either dispersed or controlled. Control of the alchemical water occurs through the 'water chariot' which is the 'water orbit'.

SHI
ABSENCE OF EFFORT

The force Shi aims to teach us to understand the importance of internal force by understanding of the force Ji. The application of force Shi strengthens the development of the internal sphere. Because, in a way, the internal sphere depends for its development on the force Shi, this leads to two possible scenarios. One is when the internal force is strengthened by all the internal processes that take place and that find their influence on the internal sphere though force Shi, and the other is the danger of losing control of the development of the form. The reason for that is that you start relying on force Shi to do the work of developing the internal sphere and basically you start paying less attention to developing the internal sphere when you do that you lose your concentration and it is very easy to fall into the illusion of having achieved something. The water chariot should never stop, it should continue to support the permanent flow of water, otherwise the water will freeze over and the alchemical process will cease. If the flow of water stops, control over the circulation of qi is lost, and the process of transformation becomes impossible.

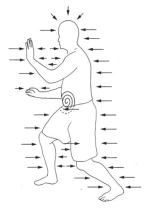

This force teaches us that whatever situation we find ourselves in, be it difficult or otherwise, it will never be clear completely to us what is happening until we form an analysis to determine its roots. It also shows that we can never be certain that we made the right choice because the conclusions of our analysis and realization may be wrong. In other words, the understanding that we contribute to the situation may not be true because it does not correspond to the right quality of energy. This is due to the fact that the foundation of this analysis or conclusion, which is body Ji, is so deep that it's very hard to dig all the way down in order to draw the right conclusions to learn the right things. That is why when this force is applied or practiced the form must be ready to comprehend it, and then the results of your practice with this form will be beneficial. However if you feel that you may not be prepared to understand this form or that your understanding is not deep enough, its best to relax. It's best to not make an effort but instead concentrate on maintaining the integrity of the form to avoid the negative ramifications of wrongful understanding of the force Shi.

MENG
INCOMPLETENESS

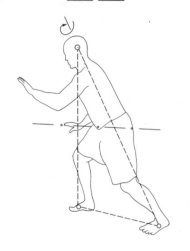

Force Meng is derived naturally from the force Shi and although the manifestation of this form cannot be considered independent and complete on its own because it simply liberates Jing energy, just the fact that it works with Jing energy is sufficient to treat it very seriously. Mastering force Meng is a very complicated process and you will have a lot of misunderstandings on the way but the experience that you will go through while trying to eliminate your misunderstandings is valuable.

Force Meng teaches that we must use what we have already achieved, cement it in our practice and use it for guidance in our growth. This force very clearly describes the connection of the external with the internal and by practicing this force you can feel the strength of that connection. In other words, you can feel how strong the connection is between internal and external. The external is always manifested by an action and the internal is always described by its content or by fulfilling some process. Even though you may realize the existence of both of them as separate entities, it is not always easy to link them together. This force does not have sufficient internal effort to strengthen this link and that's why the force from outside has to come into play. The outside force is an 'tangential' effort, one which is used to introduce changes to the form. In order for this altered form to keep its consistency rather than disintegrate or attain another quality, it is important to have a well formed internal sphere, then no matter how the external changes, the internal always will be fulfilled and will be able to affect the external through the center. Put simply, the external changes are ways for us to find another form of learning or different ways to obtain new knowledge. However, in pursuing new ways, we shouldn't lose the connection with our past achievements.

The tangential efforts which are described by the forces Cai – Zhou – Cai – Liu introduce four types of changes. These four changes occur in respect of the form itself and are independent from the internal contents of the form. It is possible that these four forces can also represent the internal sphere, but, nonetheless, they always play the role of providing additional conditions. When we say additional conditions, we mean that they are not 'cardinal' forces. The conclusion from this is that if we let any of these four (non-cardinal) forces influence our internal sphere, and we lose control over it, it will also destroy the form. (The four forces described in this book are the cardinal forces.) In the case of force Meng, the danger of a possible loss comes from a few sources. First, is a loss of Qi which leads to a loss of form; second, is loss of Jing which leads to a loss of energy circulation; and third, is the loss of Shen which leads to the loss of fulfillment. In alchemy they say that Bo and Hun souls start to destroy the body and, looking at the big picture, the reason why that happens is the breach of the cycle or rhythm; the cycle is distorted, Bo and Hun souls become active and start to destroy the body. Because in this force there is a lack of the internal effort, the influence of an external force is required and that is the tangential force described which has the capacity to change the structure of the form. This is relevant because force Meng with its lack of internal effort (requiring us to use these other forces) and the way it manifests itself — all the losses that they can cause — leads to the consequential loss of rhythm, activation of Hun and Bo souls and then the loss of Qi, Jing and Shen.

Each of the bodies works with a particular effort and each of these efforts is ultimately aimed to create an elixir. Altogether they create twenty-four conditions and only after these twenty-four conditions are in place can the true alchemical process begin. These twenty-four conditions are described by the eight bodies or the eight main forces in the three dimensions of Qi – Jing – Shen. The understanding of the incompleteness of the force Meng should lead to the realization of why all these forces have to be performed or practiced. And the reason why they must be practiced is so that they become the instruments of the alchemical process. If they don't, then your practice will not be the vehicle of real achievements.

KUN
EXHAUSTION

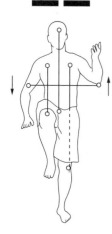

Force Kun represents the pitiful state that practitioner can find himself in if external effort is applied excessively without first constructing the internal sphere. At the same time, formation of the internal sphere represented by force Ji cannot be fully completed on its own as its development is governed by force An.

If the rhythm of practice has not been built or has failed to establish a sense of consistency in practice, sooner or later practice will wane and will not yield any result. Realizing force Kun and its ramifications is necessary because it shows the dangers of inconsistent practice or practice built on external effort without sufficient preparation. In other words application of this force has a more philosophical than energetic significance. Such realization and impregnating this realization into one's action is a necessary step for the formation of elixir. For example, in the Maoshan tradition the major elixir of 'Nine Flowers' requires that ingredients for it are formed by Yin energy. Force Kun presents Yin energy as one that helps preserve and nurture. (Most elixirs or alchemical recipes that exist are based on yang ingredients and in them yin is used only in intermediate processes.)

Force Kun demonstrates that no state or condition in practice is truly disadvantageous and can in any case be used for learning. It also reminds us that rhythm plays important role in this learning process and should not be ignored.

JIE
LIBERATION

Force Jie is the most vigorous one within the forces of Ji force.

It is directed towards ultimate realization of Jing energy. Thunder ('Ji' is associated with Thunder) liberates (opens up) the internal sphere and releases the energy which has been careful stored there as a result of practice. Alchemically, the activity of this force aims to 'shake up' the elixir, mixing components together. They say it also compacts (gathers) it, but in fact shaking reinvigorates the elixir. If elixir has not been formed yet, this shaking affects the lower cinnabar field, thus 'opening' (unleashing) it.

It is important to shake up the elixir periodically otherwise its development may be stagnated by lack of flow and the balance between Heaven and Earth will be violated. In practice, this means that internal axis will not be given enough impulse to operate and yin and yang will get mixed up.

Force Jie opens up new horizons of the Ji force and many of the previous forces will become clearer at this stage. Such is the property of internal sphere under influence of Ji axis. The 'Yellow Sprout' must be allowed to grow up otherwise it will forever stay hidden within the constraints of internal sphere. The movement is quick and vigorous, and it relieves the slackness of the sphere. However it is important not to apply physical effort, as it will inevitably lead to a loss, as is always the case where material force prevails. Form must be opened but not torn apart.

The manifestation of Kan force depends completely on how rich the pool of preserved energy is. It is difficult to realize this force due the difficulty of establishing the foundation (i.e. force must be based on a particular principle/energy/sphere in order to be effective). Hence, prior to working with this force it is essential that the foundation is found. However, even if it is found, there is no promise that it will be genuine and to avoid wasting time and energy the practitioner must be very concentrated. When force is manifested it creates an expanding effect on the internal sphere, as if the small sphere turns into a large one in an instant. This force has a liberating effect, i.e. it unleashes energy, hence control over what is being unleashed is vital to avoid loss. If a practitioner is able to maintain control over both internal and external spheres, then Jing energy gets generated and will reach the top of the head and fill the upper cinnabar field.

Application of this force aims to reach a point of sublimation, in order to initiate a new stage or obtain a new quality in alchemical work. As a last force of body Ji it summarizes one part of the alchemical cycle (one that is described by axis Ji).

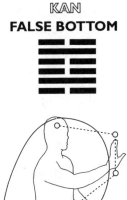

KAN
FALSE BOTTOM

CHAPTER EIGHT
The Art of Gathering

'Gathering' is the art of comprehending movements of the abdomen. When your hands move away from the body, the movement the impulse to move must originate in the abdomen. We say abdomen, but when your lower dantian is created that is the real origin. When your hands approach the body this is gathering the abdomen. To develop this principle you can use any exercise as long as you remember the following three points. This is the art of connecting three spheres.

1. LEGS connect EARTH with ABDOMEN
2. ABDOMEN connects BODY with ARMS
3. ARMS connect HEAD with LEGS

收
的
方
法

Fig 8.1

Fig 8.2

Fig 8.3

Fig 8.4

Fig 8.5

Fig 8.6

Fig 8.7

Fig 8.8

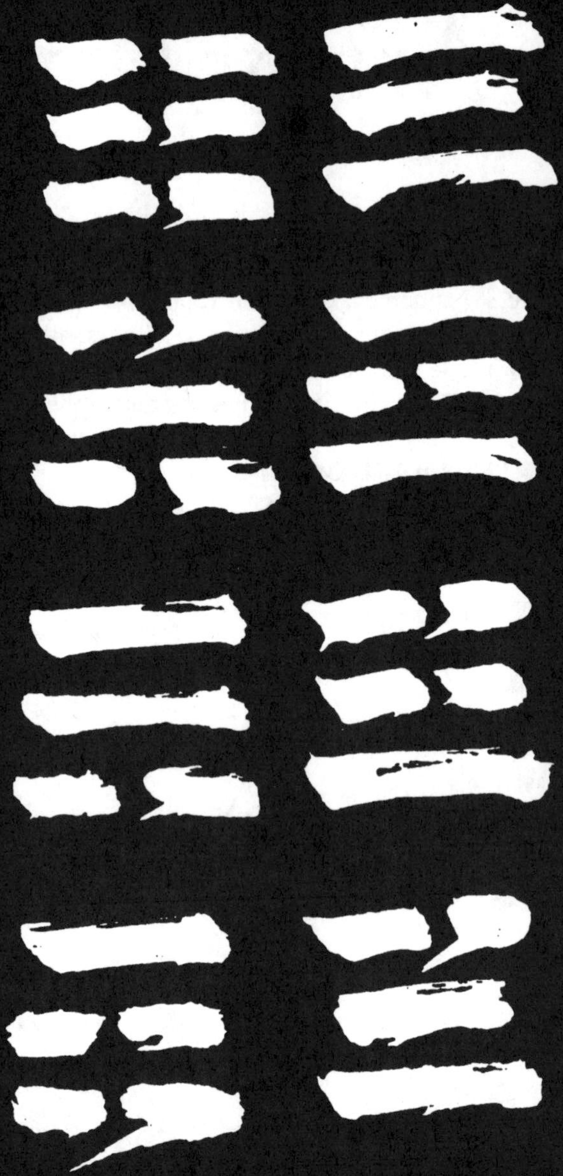

CHAPTER NINE
Creating Eight Forces

**'When my opponent is strong, I am soft.' This is yielding.
Yield to place yourself in a better position.
This is the life strategy of Taiji.**

In this book we examine four of the eight 'bodies' (forces): Peng, Liu, An, Ji. We look at them as if they are 'efforts' which give us the possibility to perform the Pushing Hands applications: Push (Peng), Press (Liu), Roll Back (An), Ward Off (Ji).

Pushing Hands is a complete system for working with energy. By this we mean that within its techniques and principles is a complete complement of methods for the development and transformation of our internal state. We call this process 'alchemy'. The complete complement of methods is represented as an octagon composed of eight trigrams. This familiar Chinese symbol is called a 'bagua', literally 'eight palms'. The interpretation of this symbol requires a deal of study, but essentially each trigram represents a different force. These forces are the tools we learn to develop and apply in Pushing Hands, wherein each force has a specific purpose and application.

The position of each line in the trigram represents the qualities of that particular force. From this we can deduce both its internal and external application. Each of the eight forces has a unique quality which lends itself to particular types of movement or techniques. We call this the 'application', 'external application' or 'martial application'. The internal attributes of each force are the means by which we learn to differentiate the sensations associated with that force within the body and by learning to do so we can work towards enriching the body energetically. Having developed and understood the force we are then in a position to apply it. Thus, Pushing Hands can be described as a work with eight forces.

The Qualitative Nature Of Energy: Qi — Jing — Shen

THE EIGHT
FORCES OF
PUSHING
HANDS:

Peng   Kao
Liu   Zhou
Ji   Lie
An   Cai

While we can say there are eight main forces, each of them can manifest itself in three distinct ways. We can think of this as qualities of the same force but also as distinct forces in themselves. As our practice advances our internal force evolves through three stages that correspond to this refinement in the quality and power of the forces. These three stages mark the transition of energy from lower to higher qualities or frequencies, from rough to fine, from less powerful to most powerful, from most earthly to most heavenly. Of course, it's not so clear cut as this description might suggest. Energy is always in flux, but in order to advance our understanding one step at a time, we can accept this generalized description.

QI
energy of the muscles
JING
energy of change
SHEN
spiritual nature of energy

QI ENERGY. Often described as the power within the muscles. It is the quality of energy most readily felt in the body. In Pushing Hands it is considered the least powerful. When Qi is transformed to a higher state, it is said to be Jing.

JING ENERGY. The energy of change. Jing cannot be felt in the body, but its result is readily visible and effective if applied. When Jing transforms to a higher state it becomes Shen.

SHEN ENERGY. The highest manifestation of energy. A state beyond description. The energy of Spirit.

Qi is a vector of energy. If Jing is the force which determines the quality of the Qi vector, Shen is the force which fills the vector up. This is their relation and interdependence. Qi is the vector, Jing is the quality and Shen fills up the vector. Each is found inside the other. We can say the interdependence is a matrix which looks like this:

QI-QI	JING-QI	SHEN-QI
QI-JING	JING-JING	SHEN-JING
QI-SHEN	JING-SHEN	SHEN-SHEN

This matrix has a corresponding relationship in the body, a proof of concept as it were, reinforcing the fact that each energy is within the other and that this body of knowledge is a complete energetic system, a system which must be absorbed in its entirety, if one's life span or one life span permits.

The interdependence of the three energies, as they relate to the body, can be expressed like this:

STOMACH, SHOULDERS, FEET	create Qi
CHEST, KNEES, ELBOWS	create Jing
HEAD, HIPS, PALMS	create Shen

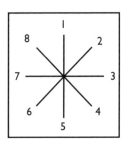

Or, from the point of view of the legs we can say:

If the feet can't feel the hips, it is not possible to understand Qi.
if the knees can't feel the chest, it is not possible to understand Jing.
If the hips do not connect with the stomach, it is not possible to understand Shen.

Or, from the point of view of the hands we can say:

If the shoulders can't feel the chest, it is not possible to understand Qi.
if the elbows can't feel the shoulders, it is not possible to understand Jing.
If the palms can't feel the elbows, it is not possible to understand Shen.

Daoist Alchemy is an internal process whereby the practitioner creates internal and external spheres. These spheres are a scaffold which support the construction of the energetic body, in the same way that the internal principles are the scaffold which support the building of the spheres. The physical body is contained within the external sphere. The internal spheres, or dantians, are located in the abdomen, chest and head. Qi, Jing and Shen are the substances which shape, give quality to, and fill these spheres.

Qi, Jing and Shen circulate through the body in a spiral manner, but there are differences between these spirals. Qi energy does not have enough speed to create itself and so must be put under some kind of 'pressure' to develop. Jing and Qi must work together to support each other. Only Shen is self-sustaining.

'Internal transformation' is the process of repetitive cultivation and refinement of these three principal energetic qualities, Qi – Jing – Shen. Because the system of Pushing Hands was originally constructed as a complete system, it provides us the opportunity to develop, within ourselves, each of the eight forces, through each of the three stages. We can take this to be very general definition of the alchemy of Pushing Hands – it is the evolution of the nature of all forces within ourselves, to their highest potential.

Eight Forces

Pushing Hands is the evolution of the nature of all forces within ourselves, to their highest potential.

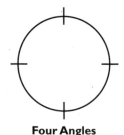

Four Angles

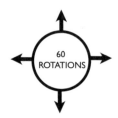

60 ROTATIONS

Eight Forces in a Spiral

Thirty-two Curves of Creation

Energetically, the stages of this transformative process are encapsulated in the following developmental sequence:

QI	creates	JING-QI
JING-QI	creates	QI-SHEN
QI-SHEN	creates	JING-JING
JING-JING	creates	SHEN-QI
SHEN-QI	creates	JING-SHEN
JING-SHEN	creates	SHEN-JING
SHEN-JING	creates	SHEN-SHEN

This sequence can be thought of conceptually as a spiral, the process of alchemical transformation repeating through many iterations. The spiral, such a ubiquitous and ancient symbol affords us many interpretations and fits perfectly with our alchemical concept here. The spiral is an ancient symbol found again and again in many cultures.

We can also view the spiral from a epistemological point of view, i.e. it tells us that this body of knowledge has a defined structure, from which we can assume a curriculum on which to base the rhythm and direction of our practice. And because the shape of this structure is a spiral we know there is no break in the process. One process (revolution of the spiral) creates the foundation for the next process; everything is connected and interdependent. This tells us that the final result depends on what precedes it and so on back to our starting point. The spiral is not only not allegorical; there are substantiated physical processes where the flow of energy creates visible vortexes, such as in the mechanism of the heart valves. The heart exerts a twisting effort which forces blood into the aorta, the resulting vortex of blood flow closes the valves, and so on. The very galaxy we inhabit is itself a four or five armed spiral. So everywhere we look we find proof of concept and should feel confident that the Daoist ancestors created their laws from their observations without and within themselves.

If you consider the spiral as composed of rings, each loop defines a complete process, which repeats with each turn. At each turn another process of energy refinement is undertaken. There are thirty-two 'curves of creation'. Each curve has a rotation organized around the eight forces and each force has four directions or 'angles'.

The four directions of each force (in the language of the Yi Jing) are: SPRING – SUMMER – AUTUMN – WINTER. Furthermore, each of these directions have three manifestations: QI – JING – SHEN. Each angle manifests a unique tension or energetic pressure. These eight pressures are the eight forces of Pushing Hands: PENG – LIU – JI – AN – KAO – ZHOU – LIE – CAI.

Daoism does not deny man his physicality or his spirituality. They are considered interdependent. Strengthen the body so that it can a perfect vehicle for a perfect consciousness.

Ancient Daoists were responsible for an elegant system through which the natural and supernatural world could be understood. It is the system embodied in the 'Yi Jing' (Book of Changes) that, on one level of interpretation, defines the nature and interplay of energy. Drawing on principles in that text here we can expose the next strata of knowledge concerning the complex nature of energy. We do this by looking at the phenomenal world, including the state of our internal energy, from three perspectives or 'axes of three-dimensional reality'. Each axis indicates a dimension of existence. The axes of three-dimensional reality are called Heaven, Earth and Human which intersect or interact to manifest the reality in which we dwell. Humans stand between Heaven and Earth. Their feet are on solid ground and their heads reach towards higher things. But rather than hold the two apart, they join the two within themselves.

Previously in this chapter, we learnt that there are eight principle forces and that each force has four directions (*spring – summer – autumn – winter*) and each direction has three potential qualities (Qi – Jing – Shen). Now let's examine in more detail how each of the eight forces finds a correspondence to natural phenomena if explored in light of the three axes. (It should be apparent that these descriptive metaphors reflect the language of the 'Yi Jing'.)

**HEAVEN
EARTH
HUMAN
The axes of
three-dimensional
reality**

HEAVEN axis

PENG	created	Sky
LIU	created	Earth
JI	created	Water
AN	created	Fire
KAO	created	Mountain
ZHOU	created	Sea
LIE	created	Wind
CAI	created	Thunder

EARTH axis

PENG	created	stars and planets
LIU	created	the 5 continents
JI	created	water
AN	created	fire
KAO	created	stone
ZHOU	created	spring of water
LIE	created	wood
CAI	created	eruption

HUMAN axis

PENG	created	head
LIU	created	stomach
JI	created	glands
AN	created	meridians
KAO	created	9 bodily vessels (*palms, elbows, shoulders, feet, knees, hips, stomach, chest, head*)
ZHOU	created	5 yin organs (*heart, lungs, liver, spleen, kidneys*)
LIE	created	7 plexus (*feet, stomach, solar, chest, neck, palm, head*)
CAI	created	involuntary internal processes (e.g. *yawning, burping*)

It is not unusual to come across descriptions of the eight forces as if viewed through a singular perspective or axis and, whilst these descriptions are not incorrect, it is empowering to know that there exists a more comprehensive way to understand them. By trying to grasp this deeper meaning, by considering all three perspectives, we can deepen our experience and move beyond the idea that these forces are simply techniques to use in Pushing Hands. For example, we could say that Peng is the force of a punch or kick, but it is far from the real meaning of Peng (as we'll be investigating further on). Likewise, we can say that 'Roll Back' is not a manifestation of the force Peng, but is a force which can help to open up your spine, but is itself one base of the force Peng.

Now let's take the three dimensions of Heaven, Earth and Human and analyze the force Peng through the window of the three axes.

PENG – SPRING
QI	a leaf opens
JING	a cold morning becomes a warm day
SHEN	snow melting, evaporation, condensation, transpiration

PENG – SUMMER
QI	leaves are full of colour
JING	a warm morning becomes a hot day
SHEN	all natural processes which create yang energy

PENG –AUTUMN
QI	leaves are falling
JING	a cool morning becomes a wet day
SHEN	all natural processes which gather yang energy

PENG –WINTER
QI	the leaves fall and are gathered beneath the snow
JING	a cold morning becomes a cool day
SHEN	all natural processes which develop Yin energy and save Yang energy

All processes in nature are mirrored in the energetic processes of the body. Spring is the time for creation, summer the time for growth, autumn a time for gathering and winter a time for saving and transforming. We can interpret this literally by working with the year's seasonal cycles, but in alchemical processes this concept can be applied in a variety of ways. Alchemical time (in the body) refers more to the quality and intensity of our internal work than it does to the calendar or clock; it does not, however, dismiss the influence of earthly time or seasons.

Applying The Eight Forces
To Construct The Body And Enrich The Energy

Kao and Zhou

The following concepts outline the purpose of the eight forces, from an alchemical perspective, in relation to our internal work.

Kao controls the construction of the body whilst Zhou controls the rhythm of construction. When we rely on our bodily sensations to assess changes, it is Kao-Qi and Zhou-Qi we are working with. As we advance our practice and in the process cause our energy to refine, Kao-Qi and Zhou-Qi transform to Kao-Jing and Zhou-Jing, that in turn transform to Kao-Shen and Zhou-Shen.

Kao is generally associated with the shoulders and Zhou with the elbows. In the relation between the two, we can think of the shoulders as the base or foundation, and the elbows like tools which help to change or improve the foundation. This principle applies equally to other parts of the body such as the connection between feet and knees, knees and hips, or corresponding parts like feet and hands, elbows and knees. We can connect front to back, left to right, up to down and side to side. Our internal organs also have corresponding connections both to other organs and to the wrists, elbows, shoulders, feet, knees, hips, stomach, chest and head (all 9 vessels).

If we look to Kao in developing our shoulders we soon realize that is not possible to develop the shoulders without developing the whole body. It's impossible to imagine using the shoulder to attack your opponent without having constructed the feet; there could be no power in such a strike. If we look to Zhou in developing our elbows, we will appreciate sequences in movement; sequence being the first level on the road to understanding rhythm.

There are three levels to the process of our body's construction and five levels of resulting changes to it. When we talk about principles or keys in the following passages, we mean the resource of all energies. What we are doing is dividing the forces into either Yin or Yang, or, from the position which can transform the forces we gather and as a consequence determine if we need to open or close ourselves. If we need to open ourselves, we can say Yang force is more important at present, but it's not possible to create one without the other, it's just a matter of timing. In alchemical terminology we describe this as the use of 'cardinal' and 'diagonal' forces. Cardinal forces are always stable; so these forces maintain the horizontal and vertical axes. It is an absolutely physical position, it is not something we vizualise. This is what knots our energy and really creates alchemical work.

Force Peng — Ward Off

Peng is related to the Jian trigram — the initiating and most containing trigram. Peng symbolizes the complete state of the sphere. In practicing Pushing Hands we effectively view everything from the perspective of Peng. Peng is seen not as a force or Ward Off application but as a parent of the structure. Within itself, Peng preserves conditions and provides keys for development. By understanding Peng we can grasp the law of energy formation. Other forces define the rhythm of development. Four cardinal forces controlling the principles are based around the Peng axis.

Jian
trigram

We've said often that as well as a 'martial' art, Pushing Hands is an method of alchemical work or 'internal' martial art. Here then are the alchemical purposes for four of the forces.

WARD OFF	*Art of Opening All Nine Vessels*
ROLL BACK	*Art of Opening Five Internal Vessels*
PRESS	*Art of Pushing Energy Deeper*
PUSH	*Art of Knotting Energy and creating the force Peng*

All these four forces are oriented entirely around you, there is no reliance on another person. If your body can be open, if your body can be closed, if your body can listen, if you can gather your body, you can use these kind of forces anyway you wish for whatever you want. And, of course, you can push someone and create energy of pushing, but for this you can use your partner, a wall, a tree or the air. This is the principle of the force; it is not a technique.

The eight forces are an opportunity to establish self reliance, this is the reason you study these forces through Pushing Hands practice. In this context 'self reliance' has the meaning of being 'connected'. To be 'connected' is to have constructed the body and energy. It would be difficult to defeat such a practitioner. For example, why are you not using your leg, because you are looking at the base of your body, in this case you must be on two legs, but when you find your center you can kick or punch it doesn't matter. So until you find or create the center, all your techniques from an alchemical perspective are only the means to find yourself.

To begin the study of Pushing Hands you must start from the four cardinal points (four forces: Peng – Lu – Ji – An). If you don't understand the significance of these we can say this:

PENG is your abdomen.
If the abdomen is open, you can gather energy and transform energy.

LIU is your spine.
If the spine is open, you can control the circulation of energy in your body.

JI is your legs.
If your legs are open, you can listen to the earth and keep your body.

AN is your arms.
If your arms are open, you can control the principles and understand the four forces.

The reason why there are so many descriptions about these forces is to show you how much knowledge there is inside the four simple things – of keeping the construction of your legs, spine, abdomen and arms.

PENG – RHYTHM

By trying to understand the rhythm of each energy, we stimulate our meridians in an important way. This effort creates a kind of necessary and productive tension between our concentration and the energy in our body.

At first it is difficult to understand the rhythm of Peng. In the beginning, when you start playing with different rhythms of your practice, in order to understand it, you will make many mistakes. It's not a problem if you don't rush. The body is slow to learn rhythm, it needs time. Even if your level is good and your techniques advanced, they will amount to nothing if you don't understand or attempt to apply the alchemical notion of rhythms.

Rhythm creates the possibility of making practice a visible creation, i.e. you can see how practice can change you. For example, when practicing Pushing Hands, don't look for a result such as destroying your partner's posture, just think about whether or not you are pushing and if you body is connected. In looking for results, they move quickly and further away from you. One day, when your body is gathered energetically you will achieve a result.

THREE LEVELS OF PENG

In the strictest sense, it is only when the Supreme sphere is created that you can use Peng. The Supreme sphere is only whole when all nine energetic vessels are connected. Peng results from the connection and combination of all nine vessels through the Supreme sphere. Peng has one direction, and that is through the dantian. In every Pushing Hands application Peng issues from the dantian and returns to the dantian. Even though all your body can be used to release Peng, it is only true when the nine vessels are connected. (The nine energetic vessels are located in the feet and hands, knees and elbows, shoulders and hips, stomach, chest and head.)

To understand all the meanings of Peng (Peng-Qi, Peng-Jing and Peng-Shen) we need to progress through the three levels. The difficulty is that only Peng-Qi can be realized physically (Li = muscular effort), i.e. we can actually sense its movement in our body. But when we can apply a force without any muscular effort, just by controlling and directing Qi, we have the ability of Peng-Jing. Similarly, Peng-Shen is when we can apply a force by directing only Jing. Peng-Shen has no limits to the distance at which it can be applied. It is the highest level of Pushing Hands — the ability to heal or harm without any physical contact.

DIRECTING PENG
The Mind of Peng

Energy is directed from the dantian. The origin of the intention to direct energy is not from the brain, but from the 'mind' of the dantian. Although we hear much talk of the dantian it is not a forgone conclusion that all practitioners have developed one. This is the work of many years of intelligently directed effort. But don't wait for the dantian to develop; for this one needs a dedicated intention.

Directing energy has three levels of application corresponding to Peng-Qi, Peng-Jing and Peng-Shen. We call this the three circulations.

1st circulation: PENG-QI
Directing Peng-Qi utilizes the circulation of the microcosmic orbit.

2nd circulation: PENG-JING
Directing Peng-Jing gathers the 8 miraculous meridians.

3rd circulation: PENG-SHEN
Directing Peng-Shen gathers the alchemical meridians of the energetic vessels.

PENG IN PRACTICE

Peng has the following characteristics: up, forward, open and clockwise. It catches, holds or keeps, saves, and controls. It has maximum realization of force and maximum control. It is neither attack nor defense. Peng is absolute Yang, absolute force. Peng is full.

Pushing Hands is like a Lego set with two players and the first to build a construction wins. It is not that you need to destroy you partner's energetic construction, all that is important is that you build your own construction first.

'To Peng others is
not correct, to
Peng into yourself
is not correct, to
do neither is
correct.'
Master Yang
Cheng Fu

Peng connects nine yang energies and all activities which create yang energy are associated with Peng. Men create a yang body by developing and connecting all nine vessels. If you don't form nine vessels you will only form six. This is because the vessels of the abdomen, chest and head are not formed. To form only six vessels creates a Yin body, which for a man lacks proper construction; it makes his structure too soft and loose.

Peng is often described as the ability to 'ward off' an attack by redirecting the incoming force so that the opponent finds nothing to strike, leading themselves into a void, their structure destroyed, vulnerable to your attack. Your Peng captures the energy stored in the momentum of their attack. Their captured energy repels them. This is a misleading interpretation in that it gives the impression that Peng is an action, i.e. 'ward off'. Peng is not a technique or a movement. It is not a force used to destroy your opponent. Peng is the pressure which fills up and gives structural integrity to your internal structure or posture. Your opponent will repel himself in equal measure when his attacking force meets your Peng. Your Peng maintains and fills your posture.

In your posture Peng must be protected from everything. If it is stronger than your opponent's Peng it can reveal itself in reactive response to attack. It is a hidden force, yet is an open force with no limit to the size of the opening. Peng is waiting to catch you. If it wakes it will catch you, keep you and eat you and maybe save a bit for later. It does not go outside to find you, but waits for you to walk into its trap.

TECHNIQUES FOR DEVELOPING PENG JING

You cannot reach Peng without passing through seven other levels of energy development. Liu is especially important. Liu is empty and you must be empty to construct Peng. But if you are empty it may not be necessary to construct Peng. This is another side of Peng.

In any case, don't play mind games with Peng. If you beat someone in a Pushing Hands tournament don't think 'I used my Peng'. You are kidding yourself. People rush to develop Peng because they want to see some powerful results. They look to the future and look past what is in front of them. They think they see the light at the end of the tunnel; maybe it is the light, maybe it is a train coming to meet them. Don't rush to meet the train because you won't have time to duck when it gets there. Peng is the train which leaves from station but no one knows the next stop. Better to find the train at station than in the tunnel.

Fig 9.1

Fig 9.2

Fig 9.3

Fig 9.4

Fig 9.5

Fig 9.6

Fig 9.7

Fig 9.8

Fig 9.9

In general, Peng in Pushing Hands is Peng-Qi. This is the Peng which relies on Earth. All activities develop Peng. How you open a door or how you Push Hands has this potential. Lastly, it is important for those on the path to note that the creation of Peng is not a process in isolation from the overall alchemical process of work with nine forces. The processes of cleaning all nine kinds of energy in the dantian is called 'nine returning rotations'. It is not explicable without practical work. Theoretically, we can do it with Taiji and Pushing Hands but it is not practicable.

If you want to reach Peng you must use Daoist meditation in your practice because Peng must develop in three directions. All three directions must rise simultaneously. If one direction rises faster than another it will change to another force and Peng will not develop.

A NOTE ON PRACTICE

Whilst we might aspire to lofty spiritual goals, they cannot be reached without the methodical progression through the lower forms. This process prepares our body, mind and energy to reach and sustain the highest level. After a certain stage our energy cannot revert to its former state; you can recreate your energy. This is the immortal path.

When you work with eight forces, keep the following concepts in mind as you practice:

1. Stay relaxed.
2. Keep soft and flexible.
3. Keep the body round.
4. Find power inside the body.
5. Rely on the dantian.
6. Control your legs by connecting the dantian to Earth.
7. Practice at the correct rhythm – use a speed you can control.

劉

丙午年八月隆書

CHAPTER TEN
Pushing Hands Steps

'Advancing is advancing. Retreating is also advancing.'

After having gone through all the stages of developing energy and body we can test our progress in movement. Movement requires the body to have a foundation upon which it can build its effort. There are two foundations that must exist for these steps to be effective – the internal foundation (dantian) and the external foundation (the feet). Beginners are encouraged to do the solo exercises to prepare themselves properly before engaging with a partner.

Pushing Hands steps can be divided into four categories:

1. Single hand, fixed step
2. Double hand, fixed step
3. Moving step (nine palaces step)
4. Da Lu (pulling) (or more literally, 'large roll back')

In stationary and moving single hands methods, each practitioner practices four hand techniques: Ward Off, Roll Back, Press and Push and develops the skills of yielding, the sensitivity of the arms and hands, plus the rooted posture.

In two handed methods, two exercises are practiced. In the stationary two handed exercise, the practitioners practice four hand techniques: Ward Off, Roll Back, Press and Push. They learn to yield by developing sensitivity of the hands and arms and the rooted posture. In the moving step two handed exercise, the practitioners learn to coordinate the movements of the hands and the legs with agile stepping.

Pushing Hands Steps

FIXED AND MOVING
   Stationary – both single and double handed
   Stationary – two handed
   Single step – two handed
   Moving, low stance – two handed
   Free form – two handed
   Free sparring

MOVING STEP PUSHING HANDS – HUA BU
   Two steps forward, two steps back
   Advance one step with Ward Off
   Advance a step with Press
   Partner retreats one step with Roll Back
   Partner retreats one step with Push

The cycle is repeated as long as one wishes, without any change in direction. Stepping must be agile.

MOVING STEP PUSHING HANDS – DA LU
   Four steps forward, four steps back
   Advance one step with Ward Off
   Advance one step with Elbow
   Advance one step with Press
   Advance one step with Shoulder strike
   Partner retreats three steps with Roll Back
   Partner turns and steps behind with Pull Down, Split, Push

SINGLE HAND PATTERNS
   Single Hand Horizontal Circle (Dan Shou Ping Quan)
   Single Hand Spiraling and Rolling Circle (Dan Shou Li Quan)
   Single Hand Forearm Vertical Circle (Xiao Bi Li Quan)
   Single Hand Arm Vertical Circle (Da Bi Li Quan)
   Grasp, Catch, Cai and Lu Circle (Zhua Na Cai Lu Shou)

Outer Elbow Ji and Lu (Wai Zhou Ji Lu Shou)
Inner Elbow Ji and Lu (Nei Zhou Ji Lu Shou)
Left and Right Shoulder (Ji Zuo You Ji Jian)
Gua Kao (Kua Kao)
Knee Kao (Xi Kao)
180 Degree Kao (180 Du Kao)
Kai While Turning (Zhuan Quan Kao)

DOUBLE HAND PATTERNS
Four Cardinal Peng (Si Zheng Shou Peng Jin)
Four Cardinal Lu (Si Zheng Shou Lu Jin)
Four Cardinal Ji (Si Zheng Shou Ji Jin)
Four Cardinal An (Si Zheng Shou An Jin)
Stationery Four Cardinal Pushing Hands (Ding Bu Si Zheng Shou)
Moving Step Four Cardinal Pushing Hands (Huo Bu Si Zheng Shou)
Shun Bu Double Pushing Hands (Shun Bu Shuang Tui Shou)
Shun Bu Shuang Tui Shou (also called Da Lu): Shun Bu Da Lu
Moving Step Double Pushing Hands (Huo Bu Shuang Tui Shou)
Moving Step Double Pushing Hands (Huo Bu Shuang Tui Shou)

Tenets And Terms Of Engagement

TENETS OF ENGAGEMENT

FIRST PRINCIPLE
  You body listens to your partner
  Your energy listens to your body
  Your mind listens to your energy

SECOND PRINCIPLE
  Feel yourself
  Feel around yourself
  Listen in the distance

THIRD PRINCIPLE
  Teach your body what to understand, not your brain or energy
  When your body starts to understand give it energy
  Give mind to your energy

TERMS OF ENGAGEMENT

I. LISTENING
  No matter what the situation or movement, always be searching for and listening to the opponent's energy. Do not disregard any tiny movement or facet of play.

2. CIRCULARITY
  The form, movements and rotation are all based on the sphere, therefore your arms must remain rounded; if they collapse into your body the energy cannot flow from dantian to finger tips.

3. STABILITY
  In fixed-step Pushing Hands, you are allowed to alternate which leg is in front, but you are not allowed to step away. If the opponent oppresses you, you must be able to sit into the posture without losing your center and turn the waist to neutralize their posture.

4. CLOSENESS
  In listening, sticking and following, the contact is never broken and the distance between you always maintained. To do so will enhance the effectiveness of your movements.

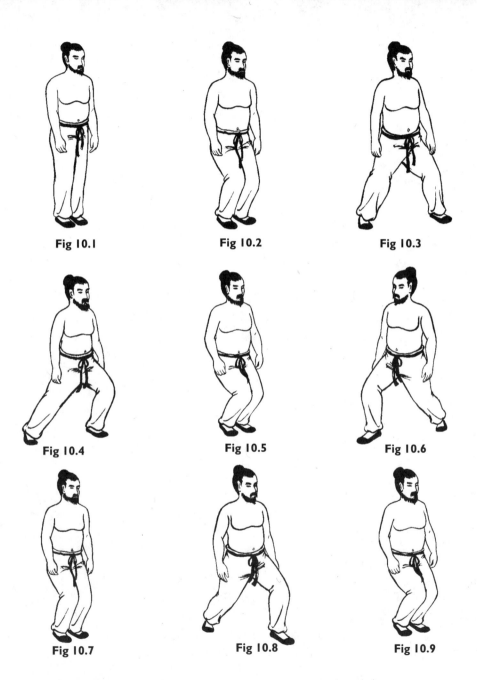

Fig 10.1

Fig 10.2

Fig 10.3

Fig 10.4

Fig 10.5

Fig 10.6

Fig 10.7

Fig 10.8

Fig 10.9

CHAPTER ELEVEN
Creating Fajing

'Studying but not practicing
is to cheapen the teacher's transmission.
But to practice without principles
is to become sick from one's art.'

In this section we can discuss more easily than it is for most people to demonstrate the explosive discharge of force that is Fajing. So, until you have developed this ability for yourself, this discussion can only serve to inspire you to continue to practice. You will learn what is required in order to prepare the body and energy. You will learn the nature and application of this force and, finally, you will understand the path you need to take towards achieving this skill.

Fajing is the master force containing within it thirteen skills (8 forces and 5 directions explained later); these skills form the alchemical base of Fajing, and we can manifest Fajing when we have acquired these skills.

In working with and applying Fajing we can define three stages through which we must pass.

1. Catch QI
2. Release JING
3. Gather SHEN

The second stage is what most people think of as Fajing; the explosive force able to suddenly and dramatically conquer the opponent. However, from the alchemical point of view, the purpose of Fajing is to gather Shen for our spiritual

发
劲

advancement. But to release Jing we must first catch Qi. This is the ability to feel the energy of the opponent (which is only possible when we can feel and connect ourselves internally). In this case it is possible to direct energy (Fajing) to any part of the opponent's body (Stage 2).

THE FOUNDATION OF FAJING
Energy Centers

In order to understand how Fajing is created and applied we must understand the structure of our energetic body and how to enhance and control its function.

There are three main energy centers in the body. They are located in the abdomen (lower), chest (middle) and head (upper). Various terms can be used interchangeably; most commonly they are called 'energy centers', 'dantians' or 'cinnabar fields'. These energy fields can be developed to a high degree and, compared to muscular strength, are the source of a more potent force. As they develop, they also grow in size and power, which enables us to sense their presence and form and, hence, begin to work more concretely with them. At some stage it is possible to manipulate them to direct energy circulation in the body and deliver stunning strikes. After some years of practice, the lower, middle and upper cinnabar fields become coordinated. At that point they form a single, connected chain of dantian which can be manipulated by creating a wave in the body, just like cracking a whip. Finally, they merge into one big dantian; the body is united and working as a whole, meaning that maximum results can be achieved with least effort.

Three Dantian
with
Supreme Center

The upper dantian can direct energy in very specific ways by changing its force and direction. Through coordinating the dantian, you are optimizing the quantity, force, and direction of energy in a focused manner and can generate enormous power with very small movements.

DEVELOPING FAJING

The dantian is like a sphere of energy. When properly developed this ball can be taught to rotate in any direction and this is the method by which energy is directed to any part of the body. We live in a three-dimensional space, so your movements should fully exploit the three dimensions, and to do so means to apply a spiral force. This is why so much emphasis is placed on developing the articulation of the waist. The vortex of power that is a rotation, twist or distortion of the dantian is the origin of movement in the waist, rather than the other way around. It's not a physical effort. Waist training should always concentrate on the internal nature of the movement. 'The body is like a wheel. The waist is like the axle.'

Whilst they sound like techniques and may be also thought of this way, they are in fact different energies we need to understand and develop along the way to freeing ourselves from the need to use a partner, who is after all only a means to check and measure our own state of development. (Although we discuss them individually, in practice they are applied in combination or even inside each other. This is the difficulty in reading about this very deep issue. Only practice and experience can be the ultimate teacher.)

The nature and quality of our internal force is what gives shape, direction and effect to our movements. When we hear explanations of these skills it is usually in terms of movement and application, which is generally just the description of Stage 2, the explosive force. Success at this stage signals our readiness for the ultimate purpose of our Pushing Hands routine – the gathering of Shen.

The eight skills can be represented as one in each direction of a square inside a circle.

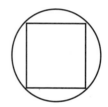

FOUR SIDES		FOUR CORNERS	
PENG	Ward Off	CAI	Pull/Shake Down
LIU	Roll Back	LIE	Split/Bend Backwards
JI	Press	ZHOU	Elbow Strike
AN	Push	KAO	Shoulder Strike

THE COMPLEMENTARIES refers the dualistic nature of each of the eight skills. Each of the complementaries is inside each of the skills.

RISING	LOWERING
GATHERING	DISPERSING
ENTERING	EXITING
OPENING	CLOSING

THE FIVE DIRECTIONS correspond to five actions and five elements. Think of them as qualities of the eight skills.

ADVANCE	METAL
RETREAT	WOOD
LOOK LEFT	FIRE
GAZE RIGHT	WATER
ON CENTER	EARTH

'Central equilibrium' is the mother of the Thirteen Postures. All postures issue from 'central equilibrium'

The Song of Thirteen Postures

The significance of these postures is that each enables work with a different energy, by exerting a kind of pressure on one's Qi. Qi is formed in the bones, it becomes trapped in the shoulders and back and cannot be issued. Jing occurs in the sinews and tendons and can extend through the limbs. Force has form, Jing is formless. Qi is square, Jing is round. Qi is rough, Jing is smooth. Qi is slow, Jing is swift. Qi disperses, Jing concentrates. Qi rises, Jing sinks. Qi is blunt, Jing is sharp. Linear force is apparent, lateral force is hidden. Void force is hard and solid force is soft.

When Jing starts to work it can catch energy from outside or inside the body. In this case you can connect with another kind of energy. For example, energy from the feet can catch energy from the earth or it can catch the energy of your partner and use it against them.

THE THIRTEEN POSTURES

CHEN		YANG	
PENG:	Ward Off	PENG:	Ward Off
LIU:	Roll Back pulling of opponent	LIU:	Roll Back
JI:	Press/Squeeze, coming forward	JI:	Press/Squeeze
AN:	Down Power	AN:	Push
CAI:	Pull Down	CAI:	Pull Down
LIE:	Split/Separate	LIE:	Split
ZHOU:	Elbow Strike	ZHOU:	Elbow
KAO:	Bump with shoulder, back, chest, hip	KAO:	Shoulder/Lean
TENG:	Sudden upward-angled Strike	TENG:	Step Forward
SHAN:	Sudden Emptying downward	SHAN:	Retreat Back
ZHE:	Bend/Close	ZHE:	Look Left
KONG:	Sudden Emptying	KONG:	Gaze Right
HUO:	Overall smooth and flowing	HUO:	Central Equilibrium

Eight Powers of Thirteen Jin

Pushing Hands and Taiji are both based on the same formula of Thirteen Postures. These are the original postures taught to Zhang Sanfeng, the Daoist recluse of Wudang Mountain, who some credit with the invention of Taiji. The Thirteen Postures 'pressurize' Qi energy to generate thirteen unique energies or *jin*. The thirteen *jin* are the power behind the thirteen fighting applications of Pushing Hands. These thirteen applications are divided into five 'steps' and eight powers. Eight powers are listed below.

PENG – Ward Off – used to intercept and control an opponent's advance.

Peng is often referred to as a kind of 'bouncing' energy. It is also considered the fundamental way of delivering energy and embodied in some way in each of the other eight skills.

Peng Jing is outward expanding and moving energy. It is a quality of responding to incoming energy by adhering to that energy, maintaining one's own posture, and bouncing the incoming energy back. You don't really respond to force with your own muscular force to repel, block, or ward off the attack. Peng is a response of the whole body, the whole posture, unified in one's center, grounded, and capable of gathering and then giving back the opponent's energy.

The Song of Thirteen Postures states: 'The source of life is in the waist'. Ward Off Peng issues from the waist, but in reality what does this mean? If the lower dantian is not yet developed this statement is relatively meaningless to us, but when all the body is connected through the 'center' this concept is not only intellectually comprehended, it is felt as a truth in the body. And this is why we keep reiterating that it is necessary to work with the basic exercises that will open the body. When the body is open, the energetic vessels full and connected, then the whole body acts as one, and the practice of Pushing Hands will have special significance for you and be a friend for life.

We can apply Ward Off Peng in more than one way; first, we use it to redirect an incoming force. To redirect a force we must be able to feel or listen to its qualities. The incoming force will have volume, direction, speed and height. The measure of Peng we exert in response to an attack is equal to the incoming force. It must be neither too strong, which is to resist, nor too weak, which is also a form of resistance. In redirecting the incoming force you rotate about the waist without losing the contact with your partner.

The second use of Peng is to prepare the ground for the actions which follow it. First we adhere (Peng), then, depending on circumstances, we can either attack by Pressing (Ji) or Roll Back (Liu).

Ward Off, Roll Back, Press and Push embrace nine other applications: Pull Down, Split, Elbow, Shoulder Strike, Advance, Retreat, Look Left, Gaze Right, and Central Equilibrium, implying that these four main applications are implicated in all thirteen postures.

捋　LIU
Roll Back

LIU – Roll Back, pull downwards. It is used to deflect and control an advancing attack. Liu is defensive, it involves soft and sticky energy which concentrates in the palms. Liu directs the energy.

LIU JING is receiving and collecting energy, or inward receiving energy.

挤　JI
Press

JI – Press. Palm pressing on forearm. Follow the energy, dropping and rotating in contact with the opponent. It is a short, explosive energy used at close range.

JI JING is pressing and receiving energy.

按　AN
Push

AN – Push. Pressing one's weight into the opponent. It can be a short or long push.

AN JING is downward pushing energy. Pushing power comes from the legs pushing into the earth.

採　CAI
Pull Down

CAI – Pull Down, grab. A force delivered by a quick grab and pull, usually of an opponent's wrist, both backward and down. Grasping and twisting an opponent's joints and extremities with maximum force.

CAI JING is grabbing energy.

挒　LIE
Split

LIE – Split. Creating a torque of two opposing forces within the opponent's body, such as stepping in and throwing from behind, or trapping the opponent's body between your leg and arm or shoulder.

LIE JING is striking energy that splits apart an opponent.

肘　ZHOU
Elbow

ZHOU – Elbow, Elbow Strike.
ZHOU JING is elbow striking energy.

靠　KAO
Shoulder

KAO – Shoulder, lean or strike with the shoulder knee or hip.
KAO JING is a full body striking energy. The Peng energy is mobilized throughout the entire body, and then the entire body is used as one unit and the force is delivered with the shoulder or back.

Fig 11.1

Fig 11.2

Fig 11.3

Fig 11.4

Fig 11.5

Fig 11.6

Fig 11.7

Fig 11.1-11.7 and 11.8-11.11 present exercises for creating Fajing in upper and lower parts of the body respectively.

Fig 11.8

Fig 11.9

Fig 11.10

Fig 11.11

of related interest

Bagua Quan Foundation Training
He Jinghan
Translated by David Alexander
ISBN 978 1 84819 015 3

Bagua Daoyin
A Unique Branch of Daoist Learning, A Secret Skill of the Palace
He Jinghan
Translated by David Alexander
ISBN 978 1 84819 009 2

Eternal Spring
Taiji Quan, Qi Gong, and the Cultivation of Health, Happiness and Longevity
Michael W. Acton
ISBN 978 1 84819 003 0

Tàijíquán
Li Deyin
Foreword by Siu-Fong Evans
ISBN 978 1 84819 004 7